WORLD HISTORY

Medieval Europe

WORLD HISTORY

WORLD HISTORY: MEDIEVAL EUROPE
Copyright © 2012 by Morgan Reynolds Publishing

Library of Congress Cataloging-in-Publication Data

Nardo, Don, 1947-
 Medieval Europe / by Don Nardo. -- 1st ed.
    p. cm. -- (World history)
 Includes bibliographical references.
 ISBN 978-1-59935-172-8 -- 978-1-59935-301-2 (e-book)
1. Civilization, Medieval--Juvenile literature. 2.
Europe--History--476-1492--Juvenile literature. 3. Europe--Social life
and
customs--Juvenile literature. I. Title.
 CB351.N37 2012
 940.1--dc22

                              2010054477

PRINTED IN THE UNITED STATES OF AMERICA
First Edition

Book cover and interior designed by:
Ed Morgan, navyblue design studio
Greensboro, NC

WORLD
HISTORY

MEDIEVAL EUROPE

Don Nardo

GREENSBORO, NORTH CAROLINA

Table of Contents

A nineteenth-century map of Europe in the time of Charlemagne (768-814)

Chapter One:

The Emergence of Medieval Europe

Looking back over human history, modern observers inevitably select certain time periods and events as major turning points. In the Western World one of these crucial milestones occurred in 476 CE, a little more than fifteen centuries ago, when the western Roman Empire, which had ruled most of the European-Mediterranean sphere for hundreds of years, ceased to exist.

Initially it was only Rome's government and the administrative system that managed the vast empire that stopped functioning. The Roman cities and their inhabitants were still there and continued to think of themselves as Romans. Over the next decades, however, the old public buildings and institutions steadily crumbled. "The cities which survived presented a sorry sight," one historian writes. By the late sixth century (the 500s), the population of the city of Rome, which had once stood at nearly a million, "had shrunk to perhaps 30,000," while "important classical buildings lay derelict [and] vast areas of the city were desolate." Moreover, "various activities at the heart of Roman civic life, such as horse-racing, circus games, and public bathing, disappeared."

As the Roman world disintegrated, another civilization replaced it. The period in which that civilization existed in Europe came to be called both medieval times and the Middle Ages. The term *medieval* comes from the Latin words *medium aevum*, meaning "the age in the middle." The people of medieval times did not think of themselves as being in the middle of anything, of course. They knew that a mighty civilization had existed before them, but they did not necessarily envision that another age would come after theirs. In fact, many of them felt that humanity had reached its zenith under ancient Roman rule. In this view, after Rome's fall the world went into decline, and it was only a matter of time before it ended at God's hand. Around the year 600, the first great medieval pope, Gregory I, declared:

> The end of the world is drawing nigh [close].
> For lo! there will be no delay. The heavens on
> fire, the earth on fire, the elements blazing, with
> angels and arch-angels, thrones and dominions,
> principalities and powers [all facing the end-
> time], the tremendous Judge [God] will appear.

Predictions of Judgment Day proved premature, however. Europe's Middle Ages continued, and they did end up as a sort of intermediary era or bridge between two other major historical ages—ancient times and modern times.

Historians vary in their dating of the medieval period, but most believe it was from about 500 CE, when Roman civilization was waning, to 1500 or somewhat later, when explorers were introducing Europe to a wider world to absorb and exploit. Of that roughly thousand-year span, the first five centuries or so are usually referred to as the "early Middle Ages." In general, this era witnessed the struggles for survival of the small kingdoms that grew upon Rome's wreckage. The age was also characterized by efforts to preserve the best aspects of Roman civilization and to live up to its enviable achievements.

The Eagle in Decline

Perhaps Rome's greatest achievement was the creation of an empire that stretched from Palestine and Anatolia (now Turkey) in the east to Spain in the west and from North Africa in the south to Britain in the north. At its height, in the mid-second century, Rome held sway over more than a hundred million people. That may have been a third or more of the planet's total population, according to some experts. Because virtually all of the lands ringing the Mediterranean Sea were under the great eagle's wing (the eagle being Rome's national symbol), the Romans called that waterway *mare nostrum*, or "our sea." Though clearly conceited, the slogan reflected an undeniable truth. In the words of the late historian Naphtali Lewis, "The entire Mediterranean Sea was a Roman lake and those who lived on and around it looked to Rome as the arbiter [decider] of their fortunes."

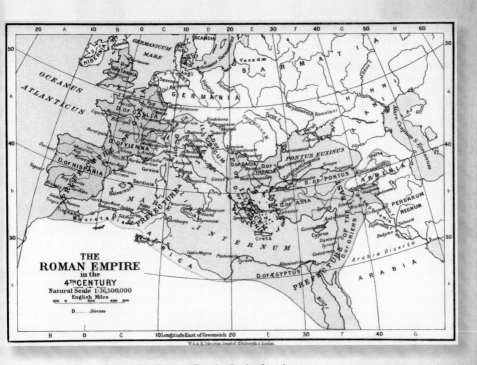

The Roman Empire in the fourth century

This phenomenal success did not last, however. As all nations and empires, no matter how great, eventually do, the Roman Empire declined. Some occasional bright periods aside, between the late second century and the late fifth century that realm suffered from economic reverses, poor leadership, social and religious turmoil, and periodic invasions, particularly by the so-called Germanic peoples of central and northern Europe. Rome became so war-weary that in return for peace some emperors allowed groups of intruders to settle in Roman lands. During these same years the realm split into western and eastern halves, with separate lines of emperors ruling each. The weakening western empire was still centered in Italy, while the stronger eastern realm had its focus at Constantinople, on the southern rim of the Black Sea.

Finally, in 476 the last western Roman emperor, Romulus Augustulus, was forced from his throne by one of his leading generals. That general, Odoacer by name, was of German descent. Most of his troops were also of German extraction because for a long time the Roman army had been recruiting men from northern border areas. Modern scholars once called that process the "barbarization" of Rome's military. The term derives from the fact that the Romans had originally called the Germanic peoples barbarians.

That slur was a gross exaggeration, however. Rather than uncivilized, those northern peoples were merely less organized, literate, and sophisticated than most Romans. Many of the so-called barbarians wanted either to *be*come or to *over*come the seemingly splendid and prosperous Romans. Both of these scenarios played out over time. And when the youthful Romulus Augustulus was forced into early retirement, western Rome began to fade away.

In this nineteenth-century wood engraving, Roman Emperor Romulus
Augustulus (right) abdicates the throne while General Odoacer (left) looks on.

Early Medieval Kingdoms

While the Roman Empire ended in Western Europe, it survived farther east. Centered in the city of Constantinople, present-day Istanbul, the rulers of the eastern empire initially saw themselves as the rightful heirs to the western empire's remains. And for a while they attempted to win back some of the western lands that Germanic groups had taken over. Between 533 and 555, armies sent westward by the emperor Justinian I did manage to win back parts of Italy and North Africa. In the end, however, these ventures came to nothing. The aging Justinian's control over the recaptured regions proved weak, and soon after his death in 565 the lands were lost to new waves of invaders. Thereafter, what had been the eastern part of the Roman Empire steadily mutated into the Greek-speaking Byzantine Empire. Although it lasted another nine centuries, the Byzantines remained largely separate and distant from Western Europe.

At first, early medieval Europe was less united, politically organized, urban (centered on cities), cultured, and socially polished than the Roman realm had been. Both before and after Justinian's death, various tribal groups began to form small kingdoms in the former Roman provinces. (These are sometimes called successor states because they directly succeeded Rome.) Among them were those of the Franks and Burgundians in Gaul; the Lombards in Italy; the Visigoths in Spain; and the Angles and Saxons in Britain. Fortunately for the leaders of these kingdoms, a few Roman provincial officials or their sons had survived the empire's recent fall, and these bureaucrats helped the new rulers to set up basic but workable administrations.

Also useful as social and political organizers were Christian bishops and priests, some of them from old Roman families, while others were recently converted non-Romans. The Christian church was one of the few major Roman institutions that survived the empire's demise intact. In the absence of Roman civic authority, churchman increasingly took on the duties of administrating local areas as well as maintaining their religious functions. In a sense guardians of civilization, these clergymen in many ways "filled the power vacuum left by the demise of the Empire," as scholar Justo Gonzalez puts it. Churchmen also became missionaries who converted many of the non-Roman Europeans who had not yet accepted Christian beliefs.

The Franks Begin to Convert

Among the non-Christian peoples who rapidly converted to the faith after Rome's fall were the Franks. A Roman nobleman named Gregory of Tours wrote about the Franks and described the baptism of the Frankish king Clovis on Christmas day in 496. A bishop met secretly with the king, Gregory said, "and began to urge him to believe in the true God, maker of heaven and earth, and to cease worshiping idols." Clovis agreed to convert but worried that his people would not be willing to abandon their traditional gods. However, he was able to convince many of them to accept the Christian deity. Gregory continued:

> And so, the king confessed [accepted] all-powerful God in the Trinity, and was baptized in the name of the Father, Son, and Holy Spirit, and was anointed with the holy ointment with the sign of the cross of Christ. And of his army, more than 3,000 were baptized. His sister also, Albofled, was baptized, who not long after passed to the Lord [died]. And when the king was in mourning for her . . . another sister also was converted.

Besides churchmen, another group that survived Rome's fall nearly intact consisted of the wealthy land owning families of the countryside, especially in fertile Gaul but also elsewhere in Europe. These nobles managed to blend into the existing Germanic upper classes and even served as high officials in the successor states. This merging of the two elite groups became crucial to the development of medieval European nobility. According to noted scholar C. Warren Hollister, "The blending of Roman and Germanic landholders into a single social order—combining elements from both cultures—gave rise to the aristocracy of medieval Europe." The males of this noble class would later become the lords of stone castles built to withstand violent sieges.

Rise of the Franks

Among the leading early European nobles was the Frankish king Clovis. In Gaul in the late fifth century, he established the most powerful and successful of the successor states. In Latin it was called Francorum, which later changed to Francia and eventually to the more familiar France. Clovis also founded a new dynasty, or family line of rulers. Named for his grandfather, Merowen, it came to be called the Merovingian dynasty. The Merovingian capital was Paris, which thereafter remained the most important city in the region.

After Clovis passed away in 511, each of his four sons took a portion of the kingdom. They and their sons and grandsons fought amongst themselves, each hoping to seize all of Francia. Over the generations these men became increasingly greedy, corrupt, and weak. They split up the realm so often that it became badly fragmented, while they also lost much of their authority and prestige. By the late 600s, most political power had shifted behind the scenes to a small group of strong Frankish aristocrats. Advisors to and administrators for the Merovingian rulers, these nobles, led by the Carolingian family, thereafter controlled the Frankish armies and state.

As a result, the Merovingian kings of the ensuing decades were mainly figureheads.

The first Carolingian to rule Francia openly as king was Pepin the Short, who ascended the throne in 751. One of the strongest of the early Carolingians was Pepin's father, Charles Martel, or Charles "the Hammer." This colorful title derived from Charles's brilliance and ruthlessness as a military leader. He won numerous battles against Francia's enemies, in the process expanding both the kingdom's borders and his own power. Martel's most celebrated victory occurred near Tours (in what is now west-central France) in 732. There he soundly defeated a large Muslim force that had been raiding Frankish cities. (In the preceding decades, Muslim armies had swept across North Africa and seized Spain.)

The Rule of Charlemagne

Though impressive, Martel's accomplishments were dwarfed by those of his grandson, Charlemagne, who became Europe's most powerful ruler since the glory days of Rome. Not long after becoming king of the Franks in 768, Charlemagne launched a series of ambitious military campaigns. These expanded his realm until it included most of Europe except for the Balkans, southern Italy, and the British Isles. He and many of his contemporaries envisioned that he had in a sense revived the lofty Roman Empire. To commemorate that feat, on Christmas Day in 800, Pope Leo III crowned Charlemagne "Emperor of the Romans."

Even beyond his extraordinary military achievements, Charlemagne was an imposing individual who did much to reflect the image of an emperor. His biographer, the Frankish scholar Einhard, described him as "large and robust, and of commanding stature, though not exceeding good proportions." Charlemagne also proved commanding in his ability to maintain the loyalty of his nobles, whose large estates were scattered across the realm. On the one hand, he rewarded them

Édité par
la CHOCOLATERIE D'AIGUEBELLE
Monastère de la TRAPPE (Drôme).

Soumission des Saxons à CHARLEMA...

A nineteenth-century lithograph depicting the Saxons submitting to Charlemagne

for good service by giving them land or valuables. On the other, he sent out his *missi dominici*, or "envoys of the master." These special agents administered justice in local areas but also checked to see if the rich landholders were complying with the monarch's wishes and reported back to him.

In addition, Charlemagne was a champion of knowledge and education. He invited noted scholars from far and wide to his court and ordered monasteries and village priests to teach children reading and writing. (Only a minority of his subjects became literate. But even this was a significant advance in a society in which a mere handful of people had earlier possessed reading and writing skills.) Finally, the emperor was a strong supporter of the Christian religion and erected the magnificent Mary Church in his capital of Aachen (in what is now western Germany).

Charlemagne's Support for the Church

In his biography of Charlemagne, Einhard said the following about the emperor's religious devotion:

The Christian religion, in which he had been brought up from infancy, was held by [Charlemagne] as most sacred, and he worshiped in it with the greatest piety. For this reason he built at Aachen a most beautiful church, which he enriched with gold and silver, and candlesticks, and also with lattices and doors of solid brass. When columns and marbles for the building could not be obtained from elsewhere, he had them brought from Rome.... He provided for the church an abundance of sacred vessels of gold and silver, and priestly vestments [and] carefully revised the order of the [Bible] reading and singing, being well skilled in both.

As it turned out, medieval Europe's first great political state was only as sturdy as the strong ruler who had fashioned it. After Charlemagne died in 814, his son, Louis the Pious, took charge of the empire. Though well-meaning, Louis lacked his father's political and military skills. Also, his three sons fought among themselves in civil wars that raged even as the borders were under attack by formidable outside forces, including the Vikings. Severely weakened, in the mid-800s the Carolingian realm fragmented. And Europe once more became a patchwork of small kingdoms struggling to survive in a hostile world.

Chapter Two:

Manors, Castles, Lords, and Peasants

Many novels, movies, and television shows have portrayed aspects of the medieval era. Most people are familiar with the images of castles with towering stone walls and draw-bridges; the rich, elite lords who owned those splendid residences; the poor, overworked peasants who toiled on the sprawling estates, or manors, that surrounded and supported the castles; and the brave knights that defended these places.

It must be emphasized that many such popular depictions of medieval society are either not completely accurate, or fail to tell the full story. For example, movies usually do not explain the relationship between the medieval lords and peasants and how it worked. Essentially, a lord, or nobleman who owned a large country estate, provided a plot of land and protection, both physical and legal, to the poorer folk who lived on that estate. In return, these peasants, or tenants, provided the lord with rents of various kinds. These might include their labor, a portion of the crops they grew, money, and/or services of various kinds. Historians generally call this socioeconomic relationship or situation the manorial system, after the word for the lord's estate—*manor*.

Most movies and other popular portrayals of the period also make it look as if Europe's manorial customs existed unchanged throughout medieval times. In reality, they were strongest in France, England, and other parts of western Europe in the early medieval centuries. From the 1200s on, the expansion of trade and other factors caused manorialism to decline in the west in favor of a more free market system in which farmers were paid wages for their work. In eastern Europe, by contrast, manorial customs survived and thrived to the end of the Middle Ages and even into early modern times.

Similarly, movies most often show life revolving around imposing stone castles throughout medieval times. In truth, no stone castles existed in western Europe until shortly before the year 1100. Prior to that, wealthy lords, including kings, lived in wooden structures. Large-scale stone castles did not spread across Europe until the late medieval centuries, and only then did they become the focus of much of the region's political, economic, social, and military activity.

Inspired by Roman Models

Popular depictions typically fail to point out still another reality of medieval life. Namely, castles, along with manorial relationships and customs, including landed estates, lords, peasants, and so forth, did not arise in a vacuum. Rather, like many other aspects of the Middle Ages, they were either direct extensions of late Roman models or else inspired by them.

Most basic manorial customs, for instance, were rooted in the large agricultural estates that dotted the late Roman countryside, especially in Gaul, which would later become France and Belgium. In Rome's last two centuries (ca. 300-500), Roman money increasingly lost value. Also, taxes rose steeply. Consequently, many people sank into heavy debt, and poverty worsened. As a result, numerous formerly middle-class Romans sank into the lower economic classes. In general, people of modest means became *fessi oneribus*, or "exhausted by their burdens." In earlier times, the majority of Romans had been small farmers. However humble their lands and homes might be, at least they had owned them. But over time many of them were forced to abandon their farms.

Some of the these destitute peasants moved to large cities hoping to find jobs or receive free food handouts from the government. Many others looked for agricultural work on the large landed estates owned by wealthy upper-class Romans. Such mega-farms had competed with small farmers for centuries.

Staggering Beneath Debts

The financial and emotional distress that many villagers and farmers felt in late Roman times is evident in a surviving fourth-century letter written to the government by an unnamed citizen:

Our community lay prostrate [desperate] from exhaustion of resources, ever since the severity of the new tax assessment had drained our very life. . . . Indeed, a field which never meets expenses is of necessity deserted. Likewise, the poor country folk, staggering beneath debts, were not permitted to bring in water or cut down forests, so that whatever usable soil there was has been ruined by swamps and choked with briers. [Thus, nearly] everything [is now] waste, uncultivated, neglected, silent, shadowy. [Things have become so bad that] sometimes empty wagons cross [the roads].

A majority of the desperate people who arrived on these sprawling estates in late Roman times became *coloni*, essentially poor farmers legally bound to serve their rich landlords. One fourth-century law affecting these so-called "slaves of the soil" stated in part, "Any person whatsoever [who finds] a [runaway] *colonus* belonging to another [must] restore the said *colonus* to his place of origin. [As] for *coloni* themselves, it will be proper for [the ones that] contemplate flight to be bound with chains to a servile status." The late, noted historian Michael Grant remarked that the *coloni* were

> virtually serfs—not exactly slaves, but foreshadowing the serfdom of the Middle Ages. Some of these men may already have been deeply in debt to the landowner before they arrived on his estate. From that time onwards . . . they had to [contribute] a huge proportion of the crops they were allowed to produce on his land, or sometimes served directly as part of his labor force. In return, they hoped to be able to rely on their new landlords to chase the government's tax collectors away.

Meanwhile, these same rich landlords were growing in number. As Rome's economy continued to deteriorate, the wealthy families that had long dwelled in the cities began to leave for the countryside. There, they too had a better chance of fending off tax collectors. And with their extensive fortunes, they could afford to live like minor royalty, ruling their vast estates like mini-empires. "The central government was beginning to lose its grip," scholar Harold Mattingly writes, "and something like the elements of a [manorial] system began to appear."

In this fifteenth-century miniature, peasants are receiving instructions from their lord.

Variation in Manorial Customs

It is clear, therefore, that the socioeconomic relationships and customs of medieval manorialism did not develop from nothing atop the rubble of the western Roman Empire. Rather, when Rome's government and political life dissolved, many of its social and economic customs, especially those in rural areas, continued with little change. As might be expected, thereafter they evolved and changed over time to fit the new political, economic, and military realities of the post-Roman age. The former Roman estates, along with ones established by the Franks and other non-Roman peoples, became medieval manors; the Roman landlords, together with upper-class non-Romans, became nobles subject to the medieval kings; and the *coloni* joined with various poor agricultural non-Romans to become medieval tenant farmers and laborers.

Although this collection of social and economic elements has routinely been called the manorial "system," that term can be misleading. One could interpret the word *system* to suggest that these elements were all alike, that they existed everywhere, and that they involved everyone in society. In reality, there was considerable variation. Some medieval peasants owned their own lands and owed allegiance only to their king. Other lower-class people dwelled in the few large towns that then existed and did not work the land at all.

Even on the manors individual situations were not all alike. Some tenants were serfs (or villeins), who, along with their children and grandchildren, were legally tied to the lands they worked. They typically provided their lords with labor and crops as rent payments. Other tenants were free peasants who paid the lord money to rent sections of his manor and came and went as they pleased. Many of the free workers lived in small villages located either on or near the large estates. Finally, not all of the manors and other rural lands were owned by rich lords. Overall, close to 20 percent belonged to the kings and in some areas 25 percent or more were owned and managed by churches or monasteries.

Manor Houses, Managers, and Workers

A majority of these estates featured manor houses, in which the owners and their families lived. (In the case of a king, who might own several manors, it was common for him to spend most of his time in one house and to visit the others on an irregular basis.) Such a dwelling was the center of the manor's economic and social life.

For the first several centuries of the Middle Ages, these structures were built of wood, with timber frames. Usually several sturdy timber pillars and beams held up the high roof of the house's main room, the "hall." Meals, meetings, social gatherings, and other communal activities took place there. Doors in the hall opened into a kitchen and pantries and stairs led to one and in some cases two upper stories where people slept. After about 1100, many manor houses had most of their wooden elements replaced by stone and some became castles with extensive defensive features. Others retained their original wooden forms or employed a combination of wood and stone.

The Children's and Servants' Quarters

This brief description of the third story of a large manor house in the early 1100s was written by a Frenchman named Lambert of Ardres.

In the upper story of the house were attic rooms in which on the one side the sons of the lord of the house, when they so desired, and on the other side the daughters, because they were obliged, were accustomed to sleep. In this story also the watchmen and the servants appointed to keep [clean and maintain] the house slept at various times. High up on the east side of the house, in a convenient place, was the chapel.

The main house was encircled by smaller buildings, also made of wood. Their varied uses are listed in a surviving medieval document describing a manor in southern England:

Outside of [the manor house is] an old house for the servants, a good stable, [and] to the east of the principal building, beyond the smaller stable, [are] two barns, one for wheat and one for oats. [There is also] a good barn and a stable [for] cows and another for oxen, [as well as] a pigsty.

Lords of large manors did not deal with these and other nitty-gritty aspects of work and life on their estates, of course. For these jobs they hired estate managers. It is somewhat unclear exactly who such overseers were and how many worked on a typical manor during the early medieval centuries. But evidence shows that by the eleventh century they most commonly consisted of, first, a steward, or seneschal. Hailing from a middle or upper-class family, he was a professional manager who supervised the entire estate (and the lord's other estates if he owned more than one). The steward also hired a bailiff, who was in charge of the peasant workers. Most bailiffs came from middle- or lower-class families that were financially better off than most in their social class. In England, the average manor also had a reeve, a foreman who made sure that the workers started on time and did not steal food or other goods. The reeve was usually a peasant chosen by his peers from among their ranks.

These managers closely regulated the lives of the serfs and other tenants on a manor. The workers toiled long hours, rarely if ever left the local region in which the manor was situated, and lacked the time and money for leisure pursuits. So with few exceptions their lives were difficult and monotonous. Yet the average peasant "was content with his lot," noted historian Morris Bishop points out, for "he knew no better."

As for the tenants' typical duties and schedules, in the fall they planted wheat and rye. And in the spring they planted other grains, along with vegetables. A few months later, in summer, they harvested the crops. The workers also raised and slaughtered the lord's sheep, cattle, pigs, and other livestock and took care of his horses. The following passage, from a census taken in England in the thirteenth century, captures a slice of the life of a serf named Hugh Miller:

Hugh Miller holds 1 virgate [about 30 acres] of land [and] works through the whole year except 1 week at Christmas, 1 week at Easter [and a few other days]. . . . He gives 1 bushel of wheat [and] 18 sheaves of oats [to his lord]. Likewise he gives 3 hens and 1 cock yearly and 5 eggs at Easter. If he sells a brood mare in his courtyard for 10 [shillings] or more, he shall give [a share of the money to his lord].

The Rise of Castles

In return for these and other labors performed by medieval tenants, the lord of the manor provided the peasants with legal and physical protection. In the early Middle Ages, the latter—protecting them from bandits or enemy invaders—was difficult because manors of that era had few or no defenses. Often the best that could be done was to hire a few trained soldiers to keep out intruders. These men were usually landless and were lodged and fed on the manor to help compensate them for their services. By the late 900s, they had come to be called knights (but they were not yet heavily armored, a development that came later).

This situation began to change when the first castles arose in Europe. The earliest versions, made mostly of wood, were constructed in northern France in the late 800s and soon were being built in Germany and other neighboring lands. They came to be called "motte-and-bailey" castles. The motte was a steep hill averaging 60 feet (18 m) high and 200 feet (124 m) wide with a wooden stockade at the top. Inside this barrier was a sturdy wooden tower one or two stories high and at the base of the hill were one or more baileys, open areas also protected by stockades. When the manor was threatened,

Right, a modern reconstruction of a motte-and-bailey
castle in Lütjenburg, Germany
Above, a sketch of a motte-and-bailey castle near
Zusmarshausen, Germany

its residents took refuge behind the stockades or in the tower, which the lord's knights defended to the best of their abilities.

A new and even bigger phase of castle-building started in England after the Normans (from Normandy, in northwestern France) invaded England in 1066. The first Norman castles in England were motte-and-baileys. But soon, worried that they were not strong enough, and also that their wooden stockades could too easily be destroyed by fire, the Normans began replacing the wood with stone.

These initial stone castles were small and not very imposing compared to those that came later. Each consisted mainly of a circular stone enclosure erected at the top of a motte. Called a "shell keep," the inside usually featured some basic workshops, stables, storerooms, and enough living quarters for a small garrison of soldiers. Over time, shell keeps grew larger and stronger and evolved into full-fledged castles. Many featured stone towers and battlements (walkways at the tops of the walls for defenders to stand on and fight from). It also became customary to add moats—deep pits, sometimes filled with water—outside the walls for extra protection. On the inside was a well-fortified central structure, still called a "keep," with halls, kitchens, and bedchambers like those in manor houses.

As the decades passed, stone castles spread across most of Europe. Many became large enough to accommodate hundreds of people, and a fair number served as the manor houses of the wealthy owners. In the late Middle Ages, stone castles became central components of European political and social life. From these secure strongholds, kings and their nobles made laws, collected taxes, directed food distribution, dispensed justice, set social standards, and when necessary waged war.

The Gorey Castle on the island of Jersey off the coast of France. During World War II German forces added modern fortifications that were camouflaged to blend in with the existing structure.

A New Sense of Family Identity

Castles changed the character of the medieval nobles by providing them with prestigious power centers. Most of these wealthy individuals began identifying themselves with the names of their castles. As historian C. Warren Hollister points out, a nobleman named Roger would call himself Roger of Beaumont, after Beaumont Castle. "Castles thus fostered a new sense of family identity among the nobility," Hollister says. "And as the castle and lordship passed over generations from father to eldest son, the family tended to increasingly regard itself not simply as a group of relatives, but as members of a hereditary line of descent. The result was a much clearer idea of family ancestry."

Also, along with the manors on which they stood, the wealthy lords who owned them, and the serfs and knights these lords employed, castles became major symbols of the medieval period. Images of these and a few other elements of that bygone society still fascinate and inspire people today. They frequently take on an appealing, romantic quality, partly because they are so often portrayed in novels and movies. As scholar Jeffrey L. Singman, the author of several books on medieval and early modern Europe, puts it:

> The period continues to exercise a unique [emotional] power over Western culture. [Most people] consider the Middle Ages a barbaric time, yet they furnish some of our most enduring [cultural images]. The medieval world is at times alien and remote, yet it always resonates within us.

Chapter Three:
The Growth of Nation-states

While medieval lords were building castles and their serfs were toiling in the fields, the rulers to whom those lords owed allegiance were hard at work forging and expanding their kingdoms. The most successful of these realms in the early medieval centuries was the Frankish empire under Charlemagne. Yet both before and after Charlemagne's death in 814, other European kings achieved varying measures of political success. All consistently tried to make their governments more centralized and efficient, their militaries stronger, and their kingdoms more unified and permanent. Some failed in these endeavors, but others succeeded. Indeed, one of the chief developments of the Middle Ages was the formation of the nuclei of England, France, Spain, and other major nation-states of modern Europe.

Invaders Spur European Unity

Several factors affected the growth and unity of these states. A very potent factor was a series of invasions that threatened Europe in the 800s and 900s, when its nations were still in their formative stages and lacking in unity and cohesion. The efforts to repulse the intruders helped to inspire feelings of national identity and solidify some European kingdoms into proto-nations.

The invaders came in three major waves. One was composed of Muslim raiders whose bases were in North Africa, Spain, and some of the Mediterranean islands. These pirates preyed on shipping and looted the coastal cities of southern Francia and Italy. In 846 they plundered Rome, which at the time was beginning to recover from the decline that had begun some four centuries earlier. At first, European responses to these raids were largely ineffective. But over time rulers of the affected areas organized better defenses, including stronger fortifications built by the local inhabitants and small armies that went on the offensive against the invaders. These combined efforts helped to end the Muslim raids by about the year 1000.

A second wave of attackers came from the west-Asian steppes (the area that later became Russia). In the late 800s a group of fierce mounted warriors, the Magyars, began raiding the small kingdoms of Germany, northern Italy, and eastern Francia. The invasion culminated in an assault by a force of almost 40,000 Magyars on what is now southern Germany in 954-955. This threat forced the local German princes to unite. And the strongest of their number, King Otto I, soundly defeated the invaders at Lechfeld. The Magyar incursion spurred the rise of nation-states in two ways. First, it showed Europeans what could be done when people came together to achieve a common goal. Second, in the course of the following century the surviving Magyars settled down, adopted Christianity, and established a new kingdom that would later grow into the nation of Hungary.

"The Fury of the Northmen"

Though the Muslim raids and Magyar intrusion were major events in their time, they paled in scope to the mass invasions of the Vikings. Hailing from what are now Denmark, Sweden and Norway, they were also known as Norse, Norsemen, and Northmen. They were excellent sailors, and their ships were sleek and fast. Also, they were tough, effective fighters who struck fear into the first Europeans who encountered them. Scholar John Haywood describes the distinctive warrior ethos (culture, or way of thinking) that drove them to kill and plunder:

> [The Vikings] created a very competitive, predatory society where success in war was the key to power and status. It also led to the concentration of power in fewer and fewer hands and to the merging of tribes, either voluntarily to wage war [or] because a weaker tribe had been conquered by a stronger. It was probably in this way that the Danes emerged as the dominant people of southern Scandinavia by the sixth century.

The first series of Viking attacks, which occurred from the 790s to about 834, were relatively small-scale. Targeting monasteries, churches, and isolated manors, they occurred mainly along the coasts of Britain, Ireland, Francia, and northwestern Germany. Also, they happened only in the summer (when sailing was safest) and were of brief duration, usually a few hours. Yet they were brutal, terrifying, and left many dead. During that period the phrase "From the fury of the Northmen deliver us, O Lord" became one of the more common expressions of the day.

These assaults proved only a foretaste of the Norse fury that was to come. In the early 830s the Vikings significantly increased the size of their raiding parties. They also began sailing far upstream on the rivers that could accommodate their

An early twentieth-century illustration of a Viking raid on an English village

ships, including Germany's Rhine and Francia's Seine, and looting inland cities. Moreover, in the early 840s the invaders expanded their raiding season to include the spring and fall. To make this possible, they erected fortified coastal bases, on Europe's northwestern shores, where they wintered and thereby eliminated the need to travel back and forth from Scandinavia. A passage from an English document known as the *Anglo-Saxon Chronicle* tells how this advantage allowed the Vikings to gather a large force for a major assault on southern England:

> The heathens [non-Christians, i.e., the Vikings] now for the first time remained over winter in the Isle of Thanet [near Kent, in southeastern England]. The same year [851] came three hundred and fifty ships into the mouth of the Thames [River], the crew of which went upon land, and stormed Canterbury and London, putting to flight Bertulf, [a local king], with his army, and then marched southward over the Thames into Surrey [to attack more towns].

In an even more frightening development, large groups of Vikings began establishing permanent settlements in the European lands they had been raiding. Overrunning southeastern England became their first major goal. The residents of some of the small English kingdoms were so afraid that they paid the invaders large sums of gold in return for sparing their towns and farms. Such bribes became known as "Danegold" because so many Norse were Danes. In addition to payments made by the English, the Franks forked over thirteen separate Danegolds between 845 and 926. In this way Viking leaders became rich while they continued to seize significant chunks of England and other European regions.

Europe Rises to the Challenge

Eventually, however, the English, Franks, and others took steps to halt the Viking onslaught. One effective approach was to unify local territories and armies that individually were inadequate to the task. In the 860s several Frankish nobles combined their forces, went on the offensive, and won significant victories over the enemy. And later, after the Vikings raided Paris in 885, a Frankish leader raised troops from far and wide and beat back the marauders.

The People of Wessex Retaliate

The following excerpt from the *Anglo-Saxon Chronicle* describes how King Alfred and his followers bravely mounted a successful counterattack against the Viking invasion of Wessex.

The king [rode] by the [Lea] river and observed a place where [it] might be obstructed, so that they [the Vikings] could not bring out their ships. And [the English forces built] two works [barricades] on the two sides of the river. [The invaders were forced to leave behind their ships and retreat]. Then rode the king's army westward after the enemy. And the men of London fetched the [Vikings'] ships, and all [of these] that they could not lead away they broke up. But all that were worthy of capture they brought into the port of London [for their own use].

In England, meanwhile, the kingdoms of Northumbria, East Anglia, and Mercia fell to the Vikings, leaving only Wessex (including London) in the south unconquered. The invaders pushed into Wessex in 878 and for a while enjoyed success. However, the kingdom's strong ruler, King Alfred, rallied his people and decisively defeated them.

Thereafter, Alfred continued to drive the Vikings back and liberate the captured English kingdoms. An 897 entry in the *Anglo-Saxon Chronicle* reflected the relief and patriotism felt by many English: "The enemy had not, thank God, entirely

A map of England in 878

destroyed the English nation!" The anonymous person who wrote that line intended the word nation in the cultural sense, for at the time England was not yet, politically speaking, a unified nation. But after Alfred's death in 899, his son Edward, daughter Aethelflaeda, and other local leaders carried on the struggle he had started. And when the last Viking leader on English soil was slain in 954, the English were at last a single, unified people. As in Germany, Francia, and other parts of Europe, strong native rulers had risen to the challenge and unified both peoples and regions. The late historian C. Warren Hollister, a leading authority on medieval Europe, points out that in many places,

> The invasions had the effect of augmenting royal power. The German monarchy, after a period of relative weakness, underwent a spectacular recovery in the tenth century, while in England the hammer blows of the Danes had the ultimate result of unifying the several Anglo-Saxon states into a single kingdom. In short, Europeans submitted to whatever leadership could provide an effective defense.

The Centralization of Power

Another crucial factor in the rise of Europe's nations was the growth of centralized government and institutions that fostered feelings of mutual aims and nationalism. Once again, England was a prime example. In 1066, William I (the "Conqueror") of Normandy, in northwestern France, crossed the English Channel and defeated the Anglo-Saxons at Hastings. The new kingdom William fashioned in the wake of his victory had a more centralized, efficient government than the one it replaced. His reign and those of his sons, William II and Henry I, saw the growth of numerous administrative institutions, ranging

William the Conqueror

from local courts to well-organized tax collection. The latter brought a great deal of money into the government's coffers. And that became an incentive for still more centralization of government. In Hollister's words, "The Norman kings discovered that strong government was good business."

Conversely, the growth of commercial businesses, trade, and market-driven economies centered in towns made it easier for rulers to consolidate power and build more cohesive countries. In the late Middle Ages, noted scholar Donald Kagan explains:

> The increasingly important towns began to ally with the king. Loyal business-wise townspeople, not the nobility and the clergy, staffed the royal offices and became the king's lawyers, bookkeepers, military tacticians, and foreign diplomats. It was this new alliance between king and town that finally . . . made possible the rise of sovereign [nation-]states. In a sovereign state, the power of taxation, war-making, and law enforcement [was] concentrated in the monarch and exercised by his chosen agents. [So they] became national rather than merely regional matters.

This centralization of power continued. And over the years the English government favored institutions that gave people of all social classes the feeling of being a single people, that is, of being "English." Chief among these institutions was Parliament. It evolved from the so-called "great council," a periodic meeting in which nobles and leading clergy discussed issues of the day. They advised the king of their conclusions and desires and he decided whether or not to act on them.

These meetings became more inclusive when King Edward I called one in 1295. Later dubbed the "Model Parliament," it included not only aristocrats and clergy, but also two representatives from each town and county. These lesser members, called "commons," were elected by their fellow citizens. In the centuries that followed, Parliament, a legislature made up partly of ordinary Englishmen, became increasingly powerful. (In early modern times it actually exceeded the king's authority.)

A Series of Strong Monarchs

France, as Francia was coming to be called, also had a medieval council that included delegates of the nobility, clergy, and towns—the Estates General. However, it met infrequently and for a long time had little effect on royal decisions and authority. As a result, the French nation came together mainly through the efforts of a series of strong monarchs. Belonging to the Capetian dynasty, founded in 987, they included Louis VI, who brought the competing nobles together under his command; his grandson, Philip II, who employed special agents, as Charlemagne had, to keep the nobles in line; and Philip IV, who made France, already Europe's most populous state, its leading economic power by the early 1300s.

The Capetian rulers also fostered feelings of French nationalism by working to expel the English from France. Ever since the Norman conquest, England had controlled small sections of France, and when the English king Edward III laid claim to the French throne in 1328, the French balked. War broke out between the two great powers in 1337. Lasting until 1453, the long conflict came to be called the Hundred Years' War.

At first, despite their numerical and economic superiority, the French did not fare well. They lost two major battles to their opponents at Crécy in 1346 and Poitiers in 1356. Yet the French persevered and eventually rebounded. The high point of their success came during the reign of their king Charles VII in the early 1400s. With the aid of a seventeen-year-old girl named Jeanne d'Arc (Joan of Arc), who inspired the French soldiers with her courage and audacity, Charles's forces won a string of impressive victories. By 1453 they had at last achieved the national goal of driving the English from French soil. "The political and social consequences were lasting," Kagan writes. "Although the war had devastated France, it also wakened the giant of French nationalism and hastened the [transformation of France into] a centralized state."

Joan of Arc is considered a national heroine of France and was beatified as a Catholic saint. A peasant girl born in eastern France who claimed Divine guidance, she led the French army to several important victories during the Hundred Years' War. Captured by the Burgundians, she was sold to the English, who tried her in an ecclesiastical court and sentenced her to be burned at the stake. At the time of her death Joan of Arc was nineteen years old. This 1843 oil painting, *Joan of Arc's Death at the Stake* by Hermann Stilke, imagines the scene of her execution. The painting, on display at the Heritage Museum in St. Petersburg, Russia, is part of a triptych entitled *The Life of Joan of Arc*.

England and France were not the only European states to follow this somewhat tortuous path to nationhood. But they were the first and became the chief models for most of those that came later. As scholar Anne Fremantle phrases it, "In their separate ways, [they] cast the molds of administration and justice that would eventually be followed in countries all over Europe."

Spain's Visionary Monarchs

Following England's and France's lead, Spain also became a strong nation-state in late medieval times. The creation of the Spanish nation was chiefly the work of two visionary rulers—Isabella I and Ferdinand II. Isabella was queen of the kingdom of Castile, and Ferdinand ruled the smaller neighboring realm of Aragon. Even as a child, Isabella dreamed of uniting and ruling the two kingdoms, along with two others, Navarre and Granada (a Muslim state). Those four medieval kingdoms occupied the Iberian Peninsula along with a fifth, Portugal. Isabella began working toward her goal by marrying Ferdinand in 1469. They ruled their two kingdoms together and later went on to conquer Granada and to absorb Navarre. By 1512, Isabella's dream of national unity had become reality. Spain was a robust young nation ready to contend with France, England, and other leading countries for influence and power in Europe and beyond.

These sculptures of Ferdinand II of Aragon and Isabella I of Castile are in the Hall of Monarchs at Segovia Castle.

Chapter Four:

The Rise of Towns and Urban Life

In the late Middle Ages, as Europe's nations were expanding in territory and creating stronger, more centralized governments, their economies and populations were growing as well. There was also an increasing trend toward urbanization. Many villages became towns, and a few towns grew into large cities.

The growth of urban areas was closely connected to both local and national economies. This was because towns and cities brought together a wide variety of individuals and enterprises that dealt with money, the production of goods, and the buying and selling of a wide variety of items. Among others, these included long-range traders and their goods; craftsmen and the items they created; marketplaces and shops where people could buy food, shoes, and other everyday items; and bankers who lent people money and extended credit.

Urban areas also became centers of learning and the arts. The first universities were established in Paris, London, and other cities and attracted literate young men seeking higher education. These same population centers came to feature many large buildings, particularly massive churches with towering spires. Such structures utilized the latest architectural styles. And building them attracted not only architects, but also large numbers of stonemasons, craftsmen, sculptors, and painters. Not surprisingly, therefore, cities became crowded, busy, bustling places where life contrasted sharply with that in the quieter, less crowded and hurried countryside.

The Growth of Towns

Some of the first medieval European urban areas were surviving Roman towns. After the empire's collapse, a majority had shrunk in size and lost most of their communal institutions and amenities (government services, bathhouses, public games, and so forth). Rome itself was the most prominent example, which by the year 600 had less than one-twentieth of its former population. Other early towns grew from villages that sprang up on or near the large rural manors in the first few medieval centuries.

A majority of these early towns were very small by later, and especially modern, standards. Populations of 500 to 1,000 were fairly typical, and the largest had only a few thousand residents. Villages, too, usually had from a few hundred to a thousand people. But as Jeffrey Singman, an authority on life in medieval towns, points out:

> A town was distinguished from a village not by its size but by its facilities. The town would have a large open area that served as a marketplace, as well as a range of tradesmen's shops not represented in a village, and in many cases [towns] also had establishments catering to travelers.

High Walls for Protection

Most medieval cities were surrounded by defensive walls to keep the citizens safe from brigands and enemy soldiers. In the early Middle Ages, such walls were made of wood but over time these were replaced by stone. In the late 1100s, for example, France's King Philip II erected a stone wall around Paris. It was six to ten feet (two to three meters) thick and more than thirty feet (nine meters) high, with walkways at the top and guard towers at intervals of two hundred feet (sixty-one meters).

A photograph of the walls and towers of the medieval city of Carcassone, France. The Wall of Philip in Paris was a similar structure.

Most medieval towns remained small for centuries, although a few, including Paris, London, Seville (in Spain), and Milan and Florence (in Italy), grew slowly over time. After 1000, however, urban growth accelerated across most of Europe. And in the late Middle Ages, as the continent's population expanded, towns and cities kept pace. In 1100, Paris, Florence, Milan, and Seville each had roughly 25,000 people, while London had perhaps 10,000. Only two centuries later, in 1300, Paris and Milan had populations of at least 100,000, and those of Florence, Milan, and London likely exceeded 50,000.

Layout and Housing

Medieval towns were largely self-sufficient. People had most of what they needed, including churches for worship and shops and marketplaces to buy food and nearly everything that they did not make themselves. A Londoner named William Fitz-Stephen described some of the diverse food shops in his city in the 1100s:

> On the riverbank [there is] a public cook shop. There, eatables are to be found every day, according to the season, dishes of meat . . . great and small fish, coarser meats for the poor, more delicate for the rich, of game fowls, and small birds.

Smaller towns had fewer shops but featured a central marketplace filled with makeshift vendors' stalls very similar to those in ancient Roman towns. Leading away from the marketplace were winding streets lined with houses of varying sizes. Most were small because they were occupied by members of the lower classes, who made up the bulk of the population. A typical poor townhouse was a one-story cottage that would today be classified as a shack. In many ways similar to a rural peasant hut of the time, it was ten to fifteen feet wide, with a modest sized main room in front and one or two tiny bedrooms in back. A fireplace in the front room provided warmth and a place to cook.

Structurally the cottage consisted mostly of simple, perishable materials. The walls were generally made of wattle, small tree branches interwoven to form a basket-like surface. The spaces in that uneven surface were filled in by daub, a mixture of clay, straw, and sometimes animal dung. The interior surfaces of the walls were often covered with a thin layer of plaster and the roofs, also as in rural huts, were originally made of thatch, a thick mass of reeds and straw. Because thatch was prone to catching fire, over time many towns passed laws ordering that it be covered or replaced by shingles or other less flammable materials.

Furnishings in such homes were few and rudimentary. People sat on wooden stools or benches, slept on mattresses consisting of large sacks filled with straw, and stored their clothes and other belongings in wooden chests or straw baskets. There were no inside bathroom facilities. Located outside, behind a cottage, the family toilet consisted of a latrine—a hole in a board resting above a pit dug in the earth. When the pit was full, someone dug a new one a few feet away.

As is still true today, the larger one's income the bigger the home the person could afford. Upper-class townhouses tended also to be narrow. But they were longer than poorer ones, had two or three stories, featured five to ten or more rooms, and were built of more durable materials—wood, stone, or both. The better homes also had roofs covered by costly fire-baked tiles. Some of the smaller bedrooms in such houses were used by servants or by lodgers who paid to rent them. In fact, some well-to-do individuals earned hefty incomes by buying several houses, living in one, and renting out rooms or entire floors in the others.

One thing that both rich and poor residents of the towns had in common were small patches of open ground behind the houses, where they grew flowers and/or vegetables and herbs.

People of all incomes and social classes also shared poor sanitary conditions. They regularly dumped refuse into the streets, which produced horrible odors and bred disease and germs. (At the time, the existence of germs and the causes of disease were unknown.) According to Singman:

> Inadequate drainage meant that towns were often subject to flooding, so that waste in the streets could easily contaminate the drinking water. [Also] horses, oxen, and donkeys were common in the streets [and] many houses kept pigs, dogs, and poultry, [all of which dropped feces far and wide]. The concentrated population supported other animals even less subject to human control. Rats and mice were common, as were flies, fleas, and lice, all agents for the propagation of disease.

Merchants and Traders

In the first century or two following western Rome's disintegration, trade among regions and kingdoms in Europe was small-scale, patchy, and risky. Bandits were widespread, and the powerful landowners who controlled the countryside exacted heavy tolls from traders (traveling merchants). As political and social conditions became more stable, however, trade increased. Also, the rapid growth of towns in the later medieval centuries increased demand for goods and stimulated still more trade.

Within the towns, many residents were merchants and craftsmen. Some only manufactured products, others only sold them, and large numbers did both. The poorer merchants were peddlers who sold secondhand goods in the streets. In contrast, higher-class merchants owned and ran shops stocked with merchandise made by themselves or other local craftsmen; food grown on nearby farms; and products from other cities and lands supplied by long-distance traders. Merchants generated much of the economic success of medieval towns and cities, especially in the last few medieval centuries. This reality was not lost on an Italian merchant who bragged in 1458:

> The dignity and office of merchants is great. [The] advancement of public welfare is a very honorable purpose [and] the advancement, the comfort, and the health of [peoples] to a large extent proceed from [the efforts of] merchants. . . . Mercantile business and activity [also] brings about an abundance of money, jewels, gold, silver, and all kinds of metals. [No] other rank of men enjoy[s] as much reputation or credit as a good merchant.

Along with a higher volume of trade, the later Middle Ages witnessed more diversity and specialization among merchants and craftsmen. This helped to promote the establishment of professional guilds in towns. There were guilds for weavers, shoemakers, grocers, metalworkers, candle-makers, and many other occupations. These organizations looked after members' financial interests and sometimes got together and set fair prices on raw materials. Guilds were also social and charitable groups that helped members who had lost their jobs or become too old or too ill to work. In addition, guilds paid for the funerals of members whose relatives could not afford them.

A hand-colored woodcut of the seal of the Merchant Guild of Gloucester, England, circa 1200

Universities and Cathedrals

In addition to merchants, craftsmen, and guilds, the expanding late medieval towns and cities became known for their universities and cathedrals. In earlier centuries, very few young people went to school and most of those who did belonged to the upper classes. They usually attended class in churches and monasteries, where they learned reading, writing, simple math, and the Bible.

Over time, a few of these church-based schools, located in urban centers, grew into Europe's first universities. Among the more famous were the universities of Paris, Padua (in Italy), and Oxford (in England). By the 1300s, some universities were run by laypersons (non-churchmen) and offered degrees in subjects such as law and medicine. All of the students were male, as it was seen as unnecessary and unseemly for females to acquire higher learning.

The university buildings frequently stood in the shadows of huge stone cathedrals whose towering summits could be seen for miles. The men who designed and oversaw construction of these imposing structures did not draw up precise

A Father's Advice

In 1315, a worried father sent a letter to his two sons, who were away studying at the University of Toulouse, in southwestern France. Among other things, he advised:

Beware of eating too much and too often, especially during the night. Avoid eating raw onions in the evening, [as] they dull the intellect. . . . Sufficient and natural sleep is to sleep for a fourth part of a natural day [because] to do otherwise is to pervert nature. [Also] Don't sleep in winter with cold feet, but first warm them at the fire [and] in summer don't sleep with bed slippers on your feet.

A 1575 engraving of Oxford, England

blueprints as modern architects do. Instead, a so-called master-builder envisioned how the proposed building should look in his mind's eye and perhaps did a few rough sketches. Then he made sure it would turn out the way he wanted by closely supervising all steps in the construction process.

For a few centuries, the builders utilized an architectural style later called Romanesque. As its name suggests, many of its features resembled those of large Roman buildings, including trademarks of Roman construction such as the arch. Eventually, medieval builders developed a new architectural style—Gothic. It features large stained-glass windows that flood the church's interior with light; tall pointed spires that seem to reach for the heavens; and flying buttresses along the sides. (A flying buttress is a sort of stone half-arch that pushes inward against the outside walls to keep the building's heavy upper sections from collapsing.)

Gothic churches first appeared in France in the twelfth century and continued to arise in Europe for several more centuries. The most famous example is the magnificent Notre Dame Cathedral in Paris. It is almost one and a half football fields long, and its twin front towers are each 226 feet (69 m) high and accessed by a staircase with 380 steps.

Notre Dame Cathedral in Paris. The flying buttresses are at the rear of the church (right side of photo).

This copper engraving made by poet and artist William Blake depicts Chaucer's Canterbury pilgrims setting out on their voyage.

Men and Women

Both men and women attended these churches with equal faith in and love for God. However, the two genders were not nearly so equal in medieval town life (nor in rural life). This was because families in Europe's Middle Ages were decidedly male-dominated. Fathers arranged marriages for their children. And nearly all family decisions about business, social matters, inheritance, and so forth were made by men. This reflected the fact that nearly all of society's political and religious authority figures were men.

Women's lesser status stemmed from the prevailing view that they were inherently inferior to men. Churchmen reinforced this idea, saying that women needed to know their place and obey their fathers and husbands. Many women accepted this subordinate role and even embraced it. Christine de Pisan, an upper-class French lady of the early 1400s, wrote that a woman should cater to her husband in every way possible:

She ought to ensure that her husband's garments and other things are kept clean, for the good grooming of the husband is the honor of the wife. She should ensure that he is well served and his peace and quiet are uninterrupted [and] be cheerful to him all the time.

Not all medieval women were so submissive and obedient. Indeed, some, especially in the lower classes, were outspoken and demanding. The wife of Bath in poet Geoffrey Chaucer's *Canterbury Tales*, penned in the 1300s, is a good example. She is free-spirited and resistant to being controlled. Of her five husbands, she says, "I had them wholly in my hand and had all their land, [so] why should I bother to please them, unless it were for my profit and pleasure? I ruled them."

However, even independent-minded women like the wife of Bath had few legal rights. If a woman was unhappy in her marriage, for instance, there was little she could do about it because the church prohibited divorce. Moreover, wife-beating was widely condoned and even supported by law in some towns. In the 1200s the French town of Villefranche passed a law stating: "All [male] inhabitants [have] the right to beat their wives, provided they do not kill them thereby."

Not all medieval men were abusive husbands. Yet the vast majority of women were locked into stereotypical, socially expected roles. Among other duties, lower-class women cooked and cleaned and upper-class ones managed their servants and tended their gardens. Sadly for them, women's liberation was many centuries in the future.

Chapter Five:
Knights, Crusaders, and Warfare

One way that Europe's monarchs exercised their growing power and authority was to organize large-scale military expeditions. The biggest consisted of a series of campaigns known collectively as the Crusades, lasting from 1095 to 1291. The European kings and their soldiers had a common enemy during these forays to the Middle East. That enemy was Muslims who were interfering with Christian pilgrimages to Jerusalem and other places in Palestine that Europeans viewed as holy.

But Europe's expanding nation-states increasingly fought among themselves as well. Their motivation was most often to strengthen their power and influence and expand their territory. The Hundred Years' War, fought between France and England beginning shortly after the Crusades, was the longest and bloodiest example.

These late medieval conflicts utilized techniques and devices of warfare that had been slowly but steadily evolving since Rome's fall. Among them were mounted knights, increased use of armor, a lethal array of siege tactics, and artillery, including cannons. In addition, a strong military culture that glorified high-status soldiers, especially knights, developed. One element of that culture was a special, highly formal relationship between noblemen and knights that later came to be called "feudal."

"Christ Commands It!"

No conflicts fought during the Middle Ages exemplified the warlike impulses of the national and religious leaders of the period more than their multiple attempts to liberate the Holy Land. The Crusades began when Pope Urban II made a fateful decision. The city of Jerusalem and the region surrounding it had been ruled by Arab Muslims since 638. Yet Christian visitors to the sacred sites had not encountered any trouble until 1071. In that year a different Muslim group, the Seljuk Turks, seized Jerusalem and started taxing and abusing the European pilgrims.

Intending to halt what he saw as an assault on the Christian faith, in 1095 Urban called upon Europe's nobles to drive the Muslims out of Palestine. In a speech delivered in the French town of Clermont, he urged Christian men, both rich and poor, to "expel that wicked race from our Christian lands before it is too late" because "Christ commands it!" He added, "O what a shame if a people so despised, degenerate, and enslaved by demons would thus overcome a people endowed with the trust of almighty God."

This map from the early twentieth century details the eastward
routes taken by Europeans during the First Crusade.

As Urban's words spread across Europe, large numbers of devout people answered his call. Approximately 35,000 fighting men joined military contingents organized variously by dukes, other nobles, and priests. These troops besieged and captured Jerusalem in July 1099. A member of one of the French contingents recalled the climactic moment, writing: "With trumpets sounding [and] amid great commotion and shouting, 'God help us,' the [Crusaders] entered the city." The European soldiers proceeded to slaughter thousands of people unnecessarily. Then they established some small Christian realms in the area, including the County of Tripoli, Principality of Antioch, and Latin Kingdom of Jerusalem. Together they became known as the Outremer, or "lands overseas."

What was later dubbed the First Crusade turned out to be by far the most successful. Muslim forces retook Jerusalem in 1187 and assaulted the Outremer. So in the years that followed, more expeditions went to the Holy Land with the goal of reversing enemy gains and making the region permanently Christian.

The Third Crusade

Soon after the colorful Muslim general Saladin captured Jerusalem in October 1187, a group of European leaders launched the Third Crusade, which lasted from 1189 to 1192. The best-known of these Christian nobles were England's King Richard I, frequently called the "Lionheart," and France's King Philip II. After the two monarchs reached Palestine, they quarreled and Philip went home. Richard managed to seize some sectors of the Holy Land but was unable to take Jerusalem from Saladin.

In the end, none of these military missions were able to win back the holy sites. Moreover, all of the Outremer states were in Muslim hands by 1291. In one modern scholar's view, "Two centuries of death and destruction had been for nothing."

Heinous Butchery

Yet it would be a mistake to attribute the Crusaders' overall failure to a lack of military zeal and skills. That failure was due mainly to poor leadership, organization, and planning, whereas on the battlefield itself many of the European soldiers fought with great proficiency and eagerness. Medieval Europe had inherited its military traditions from the ancient Greeks and Romans. And those peoples' war practices and attitudes, which have personified Western armies ever since, combined boldness and fierceness with a desire to win at all costs. As noted military historian Victor Davis Hanson puts it:

> It is this Western desire for a single, magnificent collision of [soldiers], for brutal killing with edged weapons on a battlefield, [that typified the medieval soldier], a figure who more than any other in European history was enamored [in love] with classical armament and a desire to kill at close range.

Indeed, the medieval period witnessed example after example of this ferocity and intenseness in battle. Only a few included screaming, ax-wielding Viking warriors; the reckless bravery of the French and English soldiers who eventually defeated them; the Crusaders' enthusiastic massacre of Jerusalem's defenders; and the gruesome hand-to-hand combat in the major battles of the Hundred Years' War. Regarding the latter, the fourteenth-century French chronicler Jean Froissart described the heinous butchery on the field of Crécy in 1346:

> The sharp [English] arrows ran into the [knights]
> and into their horses, and many fell [into heaps]
> and could not rise again [and numerous English
> soldiers] went afoot with great knives and went
> among the [fallen knights] and slew and mur-
> dered many as they lay on the ground.

Knights In and Out of Battle

Froissart's passage mentions knights on horses, or cavalry, and foot soldiers, or infantry. Of these two broad categories of medieval fighter, knights were the most prestigious and feared. It is important to emphasize that the fully armored knight of Froissart's era was a late medieval development. Early medieval cavalrymen wore light armor made of mail (or chain-mail), rows of iron rings or scales riveted or sewn together to form a heavy protective shirt. They fought with swords, spears, and occasionally bows. And they hardly ever engaged in frontal charges on an enemy. Rather, they guarded traveling foot soldiers, chased down escaping enemies, and in battle most often dismounted and fought on foot.

During the period from about 1000 to 1450, however, knights slowly but steadily became more heavily armored. Their mail shirts became longer and heavier and finally were replaced by weighty metal-plated body armor. These cavalrymen also dispensed with spears and bows. Late medieval knights wielded large iron swords and lances measuring ten to twelve feet long. They and their horses, also wearing armor, were a frightening and formidable force in a charge against opposing infantry.

These later, armored knights tended to be well-to-do. This was partly because buying and maintaining horses was costly. A knight's armor was also expensive and way beyond the reach of the average infantryman. In addition, as the elite military men of the age, knights had high social status. People viewed them as fearsome and gallant. Also, many upper-class women idolized them, and singers called minstrels composed songs

A Norman knight dressed in chain mail and helmet
and armed with a spear and shield

in their honor. In addition, in the late Middle Ages knights
in France, England, and a few other places took part in a
special ceremony in which a king or other noble granted a
distinguished soldier the status or office of knighthood. By
the late 1200s these quasi-military rituals had become important social events.

An illustration of the knighting of Roland, the hero of the
French epic poem *The Song of Roland*

Dubbing a Man a Knight

Ceremonies in which high-placed lords dubbed men knights
varied somewhat from one part of Europe to another. But in
most cases the would-be knight began by giving his sword to
a priest, who said a prayer over it. The priest urged the man
to use the sword only in ways that God would approve of. The
candidate for knighthood then received a spur to wear when
fighting and a new, richly ornamented sword from the lord
in charge of the ceremony. Finally, that nobleman placed his
hand on the candidate's head or shoulder and spoke these or
similar words: "Knight, God grant you a life of honor, that
you may be a [man of great trust and worth] in thought, word,
and deed."

As a result, over time a glamorous culture of chivalry—a code of bravery, courtesy, and personal honor—grew up around the knightly class. However, although some knights may have lived up to this ideal, modern historians point out that others did not. Many knights were little more than glorified thugs who often fought for money rather than loyalty or honor and raped and pillaged when they could get away with it.

The Feudal Relationship

Knights and the lords they served also sometimes developed a special, formal relationship that in later centuries came to be called feudal. Jeffrey Singman, who has closely studied medieval warfare and the feudal arrangement, ably summarizes its key elements:

> An individual with military power to offer [usually a knight] gave his services to a feudal lord. The lord in [re]turn [gave] his subordinate [land]. The feudal subordinate was called a vassal, and the vassal's land was termed a fee or fief. [A] vassal who held a great deal of land might in turn grant fiefs to his own feudal tenants, who helped him fulfill his military obligations to his lord.

In the last century, hundreds of history textbooks portrayed this feudal arrangement as a vast system existing at many levels of medieval European society. However, important new studies have recently found strong evidence that this view was misleading. Not all land grants in medieval society were made to knights or given in return for military service. Often rich people gave both military and non-military individuals land as a reward for years of service or out of friendship, and without any oaths, ceremonies, or obligations to return the favor. Also, not all of the land parcels in question were owned by wealthy nobles. Frequently both knights and civilians already owned such parcels outright and did not need to fight for a rich lord in order to acquire land.

Furthermore, it was long thought that vassalage, in which a knight took a solemn oath to serve a nobleman who gave him land, was the glue that held society together. Supposedly, when the vassals of a lord had their own vassals, and so forth, it created a stable social order in which most people owed loyalty and good behavior to someone else. However, after debating the new studies, many scholars have concluded that feudal bonds were only one of many factors that made society stable. Historical researcher Melissa Snell points out:

> Vassalage was not a common relationship. Oaths of fidelity [loyalty] did take place, but the holding of the land by the free man was not necessarily contingent upon his upholding that oath to a lord. And society was by no means dependent on feudal relationships for stability. [That stability came from] an expectation that all men were subject to the king and should therefore follow the king's laws.

Overall, therefore, it appears that formal feudal oaths and relationships existed between nobles and knights, but they were not part of an extensive system existing at all social levels. The consensus of researchers is that feudal bonds and customs began to develop around the year 900 and reached their peak after the Norman conquest in 1066. Also, evidence shows that they occurred mainly in England and France and were not as common as once thought.

Infantry, Sieges, and Artillery

The other major kind of medieval fighter, the infantryman, wielded a sword, dagger, spear, pike (a very long spear held with two hands), simple bow, crossbow, axe, or two or more of these weapons. Of the two kinds of bow, the English preferred a very powerful version of the simple bow—the longbow. Masses of longbows proved extremely affective against the

French during the Hundred Years' War. Many other foot soldiers preferred the crossbow, in general use by the late 1100s, because it had greater range and force. The pikes, measuring up to eighteen feet, were developed by the Swiss and Scots in the 1100s and 1200s. The pikemen stood in a tightly packed formation, their pikes pointing outward, creating the impression of a giant porcupine with its quills erect. (Toward the end of the Middle Ages some infantry even used handheld guns, but these were crude and inaccurate and did not begin to transform warfare until early modern times.)

At first, foot soldiers were mainly peasants temporarily drafted into service when needed. But in the later medieval centuries European kings began replacing them with standing armies manned by better-trained soldiers. They also hired battle-hardened foreign mercenaries (paid fighters) to supplement their domestic troops.

Although infantrymen, along with mounted fighters, did see action in medieval times, large pitched battles employing such soldiers tended to be rare. Much more common were sieges of castles. A large array of devices and methods developed to capture these well-fortified structures. Among them were massive battering rams to break through a castle's heavy wooden gates; scaling ladders to help attacking soldiers reach the tops of the high walls; saps, or tunnels, dug beneath the walls either to gain entrance or to make those walls collapse; and tall, well-protected wooden siege towers that carried men and weapons toward the walls.

Besiegers of castles also utilized a growing collection of artillery (devices that hurled rocks or other projectiles long distances). The earliest medieval artillery pieces, the catapult and ballista (a large spear-thrower), were based directly on Roman models. Much more powerful and lethal was the trebuchet. It seems to have been invented in ancient China but did not come into wide use in Europe until the 1100s. The device consisted of a large wooden apparatus in which the projectile rested in a leather sling attached to one end of a long beam. When a heavy counterweight dropped, the beam swung into

Trebuchets at the medieval Castle of Castelnaud in Aquitaine, France

a vertical position and the sling shot forward, releasing the missile.

Trebuchets became increasingly obsolete as cannon technology rapidly progressed. Merchants and other travelers introduced gunpowder, another Chinese invention, to Europe in the 1200s, and the first crude cannons appeared not long after 1300. By 1414, cannons had become so effective that a German nobleman was able to shatter most of the walls of an enemy castle in two days. This unprecedented event shocked people across the continent.

Even more impressive was the use of cannons by France's King Charles VIII. In 1494 he transported forty-four of the most advanced cannons yet devised to Italy and demonstrated his power by reducing the imposing castle of Firizzano to rubble in only a few hours. Some of the neighboring Italian city-states wasted no time in surrendering to him without a fight. "The whole of Italy quaked at his passage," military historian John Keegan writes. "His guns had brought a true revolution in war-making." Indeed, at this juncture medieval warfare was on its proverbial last legs. And the modern age, in which most of the globe would come under the sway of Western military powers, loomed ominously on the horizon.

Chapter Six:

Ravaged by Famine and Plague

In the title of her 1978 survey of medieval Europe, two-time Pulitzer Prize-winning historian Barbara W. Tuchman called the 1300s "The Calamitous 14th Century." She could not have chosen a better word to describe that fateful period, because one calamity after another struck Europe. The Hundred Years' War, which began in 1337, killed an estimated 3 million English and French soldiers and civilians. That figure represents a crippling one-seventh of the two nations' combined populations. (In comparison, imagine if the United States lost one-seventh of its population—some 44 million people—in a modern war.)

Yet that great conflict's death toll paled in comparison to the one meted out by natural disasters. In the space of fewer than four decades, Europe was struck by the worst famine of the Middle Ages and one of the two most lethal disease epidemics in recorded history. Moreover, these upheavals created so much fear and social and economic chaos that untold numbers more died in mass murders and rebellions during and after them. All told, the calamities were so enormous that the Europe that emerged in the 1400s barely resembled the one that existed a century before.

The Great Famine

One reason that the natural disasters of the 1300s were so destructive was that Europeans were totally unprepared for them. They were unaware of the existence of germs and the causes of disease. And they had no idea that global climate changes were slowly occurring, in the process causing slow but crucial shifts in human population and land use.

For example, between about 800 and 1200 Europe entered what scientists call the Medieval Warming Period (MWP). Temperatures increased by up to almost six degrees Fahrenheit (three degrees Celsius). This significantly extended the growing season across the continent and encouraged farmers to clear more land for cultivation. The resulting increases in food supplies encouraged population expansion, which in turn stimulated the growth of towns and trade. England's population grew from about 1 million in 1050 to roughly 4 million in 1300. And in the same period Europe's overall population approximately doubled, from 40 to 80 million.

The problem was that feeding the increasing population required that food supplies at the least remain stable and preferably expand in volume. Yet farmers were already working at full capacity. So even small crop losses in a given area could be potentially disastrous for its residents.

As it happened, Europe experienced major rather than small crop losses. The culprit was another climatic shift. Between about 1250 and 1460, a rapid cooling trend, now called the Little Ice Age, set in. The winters of 1303 and 1306 were so severe that the Baltic Sea (lying between Germany and Sweden) froze over for the first time in human memory. As the climate continued to cool, the growing season shortened at an alarming rate.

Then the tipping point came. Between 1315 and 1317, three extremely cold winters in a row brought about large-scale crop losses and serious food shortages. Just how serious they were can be seen in a surviving statistic from London, where in 1316 the price of wheat was eight times what it had been three years before. Morris Bishop provides more grim details about the conditions of mass starvation:

> [There was] no governmental organization of famine relief, no system for arranging and financing the movement of surpluses from areas of plenty to those of want. . . . The church did its best with [charity food drives], but in famine country the church was nearly as poor as its [parishioners]. When the starving found a store of food, they were likely to eat so ravenously that they died.

No one knows for sure how many people perished in the so-called Great Famine, which continued intermittently into the 1320s and well beyond in some regions. Some experts estimate that between 10 and 25 percent of local populations died. Even if the lower figure is the correct one, the death toll could easily have been 7 to 8 million or more.

Hunger in the Land

In 1315, an English chronicler wrote the following about the worsening food shortages:

> Hunger grew in the land, [as] meat and eggs began to run out, capons and fowl could hardly be found, and animals died of pest [disease]. Bread did not have its usual nourishing power and strength because the grain was not nourished by the warmth of summer sunshine. Hence those who ate it, even in large quantities, were hungry again after a little while, [so] the poor wasted away when even the rich were constantly hungry. . . . Horse meat was precious; plump dogs were stolen; and according to many reports, men and women in many places secretly ate their own children.

A Deadly Noose Around Europe

Even as many Europeans were doing their best to recover from and/or adjust to the setbacks created by the climatic cooling trend, they had no inkling that a far greater menace was almost upon them. It was a devastating disease caused by bacteria. The germs were carried by fleas, which infested rats and other rodents, which in turn brought them into human habitations. When a flea carrying the germs bites a person, the bacteria move to the lymph nodes, where they rapidly multiply and form painful egg-shaped lumps, called buboes, in the groin or underarms. Within a few days, the germs then enter the bloodstream and invade the vital organs. Dark spots appear on the skin, which itself begins to bleed, and in most cases death swiftly follows. Modern doctors later dubbed the pestilence bubonic plague after the buboes. Medieval Europeans called it the Black Death after the dark splotches it produced on the skin.

In the mid-1340s, the plague steadily spread westward along the ancient trade routes that led from China to the territories around the Black Sea. Thousands of people in the area contracted the disease. And from one of the sea's ports European ships carried it to towns in Syria, Greece, Italy, Spain, and other ports on the shores of the Mediterranean Sea. The disease traveled inland with frightening speed. A French chronicler described it as it passed through his own country:

> Nothing like it has been heard or seen or read about. [A] healthy person who visited the sick hardly ever escaped death [and] in many places not two men remained alive out of twenty. The mortality [death] was so great that . . . more than 500 bodies a day were being taken in carts from the Hotel-Dieu in Paris for burial.

An illustration of the Black Death taken from the Toggenburg Bible, circa 1411

Late in 1348, the Black Death crossed the English Channel. Carried by traders, it also headed eastward into Germany and Russia. In little more than four years, one modern observer writes, "the plague almost closed a deadly noose around Europe."

Having no idea what caused the epidemic, people jumped to all sorts of conclusions. Many were sure it was a punishment sent by God. One Englishman declared, "See how England mourns, drenched in tears. The people, stained by sin, quake with grief. Plague is killing men and beasts . . . because vices rule unchallenged here." Attempting a more physical explanation, a group of French doctors ascribed the disease to air that had "become putrid or corrupt by being mixed with something else."

Attempts to Regulate Sanitation

Guessing that the Black Death was somehow contagious, officials in some European towns created sanitation regulations. Following are excerpts from the regulations passed by the Italian town of Pistoia in May 1348:

No one [shall] dare or presume to bring or fetch to Pistoia . . . any old linen or woolen clothes, [and] the cloth [already here is] to be burned in the public [square]. [Also] the bodies of the dead shall not be removed from the place of death until they have been enclosed in a wooden box, and the lid of planks nailed down, so that no stench can escape.

Another cause commonly cited to explain the onset of the malady was that Jews had poisoned wells and other water supplies in order to murder Christians. (The same charges were also leveled at Muslims and lepers.) Jews had already been the targets of cruel bigotry and persecution for centuries. And now frightened, angry people across the continent turned on Jews with brutal vengeance, maiming and killing tens of thousands. A German clergyman wrote:

> All the Jews between Colgne and Austria were burnt and killed . . . maidens and the old along with the [young men]. In [the town of] Horw, they were burnt in a pit. And when the wood and straw had been consumed, some Jews [still] remained half alive. [So the Christians] snatched up [clubs] and stones and dashed out the brains of those trying to creep out of the fire.

Still other people reacted to the Black Death by inflicting pain on themselves in hopes of obtaining God's forgiveness. Groups of these ultra-devout individuals, called flagellants, marched from town to town. Reaching a town square, they removed their shirts and beat themselves with whips until they bled profusely. Often local residents who witnessed this peculiar spectacle moaned and wept in compassion for the self-torturers.

Better Fed than Their Masters

By the early 1350s, the epidemic had largely run its course (although smaller outbreaks occurred occasionally in the two centuries that followed). The exact number of Europeans who died from the plague between 1347 and 1354 will never be known. But modern experts estimate the death toll at roughly 25 million, more than a third of the continent's population at the time.

The Great Famine and Black Death had not only killed millions, they had left many of the survivors mentally and emotionally scarred, distrustful of both their fellow humans and God. "In the second half of the fourteenth century," says scholar Philip Ziegler, Europeans "were enduring a crisis of faith. Assumptions which had been taken for granted for centuries were now in question, [and] the very framework of men's reasoning seemed to be breaking up." As a result, some people actually lost their faith in God, while others at least wondered why the deity had forsaken them.

In the meantime, everyone was forced to struggle with the enormous changes the devastation had brought about. In fact, the social, economic, and technological impacts of the disasters were weighty and far-reaching. One of the more dramatic alterations was the sudden decline of the manorial bonds in which agricultural peasants had long been tied to estates owned by wealthy lords. This came about in part because widespread population losses had left most of the big landowners with too few cheap laborers for the megafarms to continue making high profits. This proved to be a boon for the surviving workers, who demanded and got higher wages. This eventually led to higher living standards for the lower classes. In 1375, an English estate owner named John Gower griped:

> The world [is going] fast from bad to worse, [for] labor is now at so high a price that he who will order his business aright must pay five or six shillings now for what cost him two in former times. . . . The poor and small folk [now] demand to be better fed than their masters!

Gower and his peers were horrified at what they saw as uppity inferiors who did not know their place. Frantic, the nobles began levying new taxes and making rules meant to keep the old social order in place. But this approach backfired.

Insurrections by peasants and other laborers occurred in many parts of Europe. In 1358, for instance, French peasants rose in the thousands and terrorized numerous estates of the rich and privileged. Jean Froissart recalled:

> With staves [wooden rods] and knives, [they] went to the house of a knight [and] broke [it] up [and] slew the knight and the lady and all his children, [and] they went to another castle and took the [owner outside] and bound him fast to a stake and then violated his wife and daughter before his face [and then killed them all].

Similarly, in 1381 some 100,000 angry protestors swarmed into London and demanded to see King Richard II. Fearing for himself and his nobles, he met with the crowd's leaders and agreed to reduce taxes and get rid of laws intended to keep workers' wages low.

English King Richard II

This communal watermill at Braine Castle in Belgium was built in the twelfth century. Many medieval watermills are still in use today.

Technical and Scientific Advances

The sweeping social and economic changes that followed the Black Death also stimulated both expanded use of existing technologies and the development of new ones. For example, the increases in human labor costs encouraged more reliance on machines such as windmills and watermills. Windmills had been employed on a small scale in Europe for about two centuries and watermills had been exploited since the start of the Middle Ages. In the century following the natural disasters, however, thousands of new versions of both devices appeared in England, France, the Netherlands, Italy, and other parts of Europe.

An important new labor-saving device was the printing press. Since ancient times, multiple copies of books and other manuscripts had been painstakingly created by hand by thousands of trained scribes, a long and very expensive process. David Herlihy, a historian of medieval and renaissance life and professor of medieval economic history at Harvard University wrote:

> As long as wages were low this method of reproduction based on intensive human labor was satisfactory enough. But the late medieval population plunge raised labor costs and also [motivated the invention of] a cheaper way of reproducing books. Johann Gutenberg's invention of printing on the basis of movable metal type in 1453 was only the culmination of many experiments carried on across the previous century.

Also crucial were new medical advances. Medieval doctors were painfully aware that they had been helpless to stop or even to slow the onslaught of the Black Death. In the years that followed, members of the medical profession began trying to expand its knowledge of the human body and disease. They initiated dissection of human corpses, a practice that had been forbidden in Europe in the pre-plague centuries. This advanced the science of anatomy. Also, surgery began to be taught in universities across the continent. These and other examples of medical progress were precursors of the modern scientific method, which would start to emerge about a century later. Clearly, Europeans' social, economic, and technological reactions to the deadly and demoralizing experiences of the 1300s helped to hasten their entry into the brave new world of modern times.

Chapter Seven:
Mounting Divisions in the Church

Nobles, town officials, and doctors all lost prestige during the onset of the Black Death in the 1300s. Most average people believed that these and other authority figures had not done enough to alleviate the suffering both during and after the crisis. However, no influential members of society lost as much credibility in those years as bishops, priests, and other churchmen. Large numbers of Europeans felt that the clergy should have been able to mediate or plead with God to either end the plague or lessen its severity. But the general view was that the churchmen's prayers had no effect. Moreover, even some of the most devout and moral priests contracted the disease and died in agony. As a result, numerous survivors lost respect for the church.

This setback for the Roman Catholic Church turned out to be only one of several serious problems the institution faced in the late Middle Ages. Over the years the clergy managed to regain the trust of most of those who had become disillusioned during the plague years. However, divisions within the church itself had already surfaced and in time they increased in intensity. Eventually, that great medieval institution could no longer withstand the strain and permanently fragmented, forever changing both the character of European life and course of world history.

Europe's Spiritual Guide

To understand why loss of respect for and major divisions within the church were so momentous, one must first consider how unified and powerful that institution had been in earlier medieval centuries. Christianity had initially risen to power in the fourth century. In the astonishingly short span of a few decades, it had grown from a small fringe group of despised, persecuted people to the official religion of the Roman Empire. Only about a century later, the western sector of that realm disintegrated, leaving a few successor states and the very much intact church as Europe's only large-scale organized entities.

In the centuries that followed, the church proved to be the most influential surviving remnant of western Rome. Christian beliefs, rituals, and clergymen came to deeply affect the lives of all Europeans, rich and poor alike. In fact, the church became the uncontested spiritual guide for medieval Europe. As scholar Thomas Brown puts it:

> By the late ninth century, the church's role was essentially the one which it was to play [for] centuries. [It] scored notable successes in establishing a Christian view of kingship, in setting up enduring centers of education and learning, [and] most important of all, in promoting itself as a distinct, elite [institution that God] intended to lead man[kind] to salvation.

Indeed, providing salvation—a person's entry into heaven after leading a life of decency and faith in God—was in a sense the cornerstone on which the medieval church rested. Seeing themselves as instruments of God and his divine will, the early popes viewed it as their duty to convert as many non-Christians as possible. One tool they used to achieve this goal was to send out missionaries to teach Christian beliefs, values, and rituals. These hardworking, often selfless men became heroes to both their fellow clergymen and the faithful who had already converted. Alcuin of York, an English scholar who taught in Charlemagne's court in the late 700s, praised several past missionaries who "traveled in ships across the [seas] in quest of pagan lands, where they attempted to spread the word of salvation by sowing it in barbarian hearts."

A Shining Light in His Teaching

In extolling the virtues of earlier Christian missionaries who had converted millions of "barbarians" to Christianity, Alcuin singled out some by name, including a bishop named Egbert:

Early in life [he] left his native country for love of his heavenly homeland and, traveling abroad, set the Irish an example of how to live. A shining light in his teaching, he instructed all manner of men by his words and deeds. Generous to the poor . . . this godly man led an excellent life, brilliant with outstanding piety till the day of his death.

After praising the missionary Egbert, who worked in Ireland, Alcuin mentioned that bishop's companion, Wihtberht. The latter, Alcuin wrote, "built an excellent shelter for the monks of his race," where he led "a life of contemplation." This was a reference to one of the first of many monasteries erected in the early medieval centuries.

The monastic movement was a second important tool the church used to establish itself and to build new communities of converts wherever it could. Christian monasteries, which had gotten their start in late Roman times, were places where devout persons pursued lives of strict self-discipline and self-denial in order to achieve a closer relationship with God.

Among the first and most representative early medieval monasteries were those of the Benedictine order. Established in Italy by Benedict of Nursia in the sixth century, the group produced a long document that became known as the *Rule*. It broke down into sections that instructed monks on how to sleep, hold daily religious services, perform manual labor, choose the right clothes and shoes, and much more. Overall, the document explained the proper and acceptable ways to run and live in a monastery. And hundreds of such religious retreats that appeared in Europe in the centuries that followed used it as a guide.

Following the dictates of the *Rule*, a typical monastic day "was filled with carefully regulated activities," according to C. Warren Hollister. They included "communal prayer, devotional reading, and work—field work, household work, [and] manuscript copying." Furthermore,

> [monks] were pledged to the fundamental obligations of poverty, chastity, and obedience. Benedictines were to resist the three great worldly temptations of money, sex, and ambition by [giving up] all personal possessions, living a celibate [sexless] life, and obeying the abbot.

Many medieval monks read and studied so much that they became skilled scholars and teachers. They not only wrote books to record knowledge, but also frequently established schools in their monasteries. Some children from the middle and upper classes became literate and even well-educated attending such schools. When and where needed, the monks also did a sort of outreach work in which they taught non-Christians the basics of Christian thought and practice, thereby expanding the faith.

The Church in Control

Whether through monks living in monasteries or regular priests leading congregations of worshipers in villages and towns, the church was an unqualified success. It increasingly came to shape the lives, customs, and in some ways even

A fifteenth-century illustration of a scribe copying a manuscript

the thinking of nearly all Europeans. The popes and other clergy taught that Christianity was the only genuine faith. So non-believers, Muslims, and other non-Christians were in grievous error and could not achieve salvation unless they became Christians.

Moreover, churchmen taught members of their flocks that deviating from accepted beliefs and rituals was wrong. On the one hand, such behavior was a threat to the church's authority and the established social order that clergymen helped to maintain. On the other, departure from traditional religious and social rules, including a wide range of sins, was against God's will. To help keep the faithful in line, the church reminded them that God created them in his image, so they owed him their love and allegiance. On the flip side, church officials also skillfully used fear. They warned that unrepentant criminals and other sinners would suffer for eternity in hell.

A Medieval View of Hell

Various medieval people described visions of hell, many of which were similar to that of an Irish knight named Tundale, committed to writing in 1149. A modern summary of the lengthy document says in part:

> [In hell] murderers are melted and re-formed in the fires of a stinking pit [and] robbers, and more particularly the sacrilegious [heretics], who have defiled holy ground, are in a fiery lake full of beasts, [while] those guilty of sexual sins are tormented within an oven-like house, [where their souls] are hacked into bits by fiends, with devices ranging from weapons to farm implements, and then re-formed and hacked up again. [As for] lustful clergy [who] have broken their vows, [they] are swallowed by a great bird and infested with vermin that creep in and out of their bodies.

Leading churchmen also sought as best as they could to control governments and the powerful nobles who ran them. The ideal goal in this regard was theocracy, a system in which the church would have charge of both religious and secular (worldly) affairs. However, Europe's monarchs and their leading nobles consistently resisted such an arrangement. The result was a lengthy contest between the popes and secular nobility.

The church attained its greatest victory in this struggle, as well as its height of power and influence over European society, in the 1070s. An unusually ambitious and audacious pope, Gregory VII, issued a decree stating, among other things, that all secular rulers must kiss the pope's feet. Also, the pope "may be permitted [to] depose emperors" and "he who is not at peace with the Roman church shall not be considered Catholic." Gregory then issued a separate decree in which he forbade the establishment of new churches by kings and other secular rulers.

In a daring move, Germany's King Henry IV penned a defiant letter in which he called the pope a "false monk." Henry also demanded that Gregory resign in favor of a new pope who would "not practice violence under the cloak of religion." The king closed the letter with words to the effect of "go to hell."

The furious Gregory reacted to Henry's refusal to knuckle under by excommunicating him. Excommunication was a potent weapon in the papacy's arsenal. Because it denied a person the principal objective of Christian faith—salvation—it almost always proved effective in enforcing the pope's authority. Henry's case was no exception. His nobles were so afraid that they too would lose their path to heaven that they stopped supporting him. A few months later, Henry reluctantly gave in. In a self-effacing display of defeat and humility, he stood barefoot in the snow for days until the pope lifted the excommunication.

King Henry IV of Germany

The Avignon Papacy and Great Schism

Later popes were never able to follow up on Gregory's success, however. As time went on, they increasingly lost ground to the kings, whose governments grew more unified and powerful in the late Middle Ages. That period also witnessed the church as a whole suffer from serious losses of prestige (including that following the Black Death), as well as mounting divisions that sapped its strength.

One telling example of the papacy's declining influence over secular authorities came in 1303. Following some heated disagreements with France's King Philip IV, Pope Boniface VIII excommunicated him. Philip, a strong monarch who feared no one, including the pope, acted swiftly and decisively. He sent men to seize Boniface, who was beaten up and humiliated before being released. Badly shaken, he died a month later, sending church officials in Rome into turmoil over how to react.

Under pressure from both Philip and leading French clergymen, in 1309 one of Boniface's immediate successors, Clement V, moved the papacy's headquarters from Rome to the French town of Avignon. In Yale historian Donald Kagan's words, "After Boniface's humiliation, popes never again so seriously threatened kings and emperors. [In] the future, the relation between church and state would tilt toward state control of religion."

The Avignon papacy also led directly to one of the church's lowest points in the medieval era. In 1378, high-ranking churchmen in Rome chose a pope of their own. For close to four decades, separate, competing lines of popes were elected, with England and its allies backing the Roman line and France and its own allies supporting the Avignon line. This split in religious leadership, known as the Great Schism, cheapened the church's image. The division finally ended in 1417 after leading clergymen from across Europe gathered in the so-called Council of Constance. They deposed the rival popes and elected a new one, Martin V, who reigned over a reunited church until 1431.

The Rise of Religious Reformers

Reunification was not enough to restore the church to its former glory and singular authority, however. The papacy had been seriously discredited. Moreover, in the century following the Council of Constance, the popes lost even more clout and integrity. "Abandoning much of their former [control] over the international church," C. Warren Hollister writes, "they devoted themselves to [Italian] politics." Thereafter most popes were Italian noblemen who allowed Europe's kings to exercise an "extensive degree of control over church and clergy in return for formal recognition of papal authority."

The Roman Catholic Church that greeted the dawn of the sixteenth century was a mere shell of its early medieval self. Its leaders had become so weak, corrupt, and out of touch with large numbers of the faithful that they were unable to quell new sources of unrest within their own ranks. In 1517, a German monk and theology professor named Martin Luther publicly criticized the church for allowing indulgences, pardons for confessed sins, to be sold for a profit. This shady practice, he charged, made salvation a mere thing to be bought and sold. Luther became famous across Europe almost overnight. And soon other reformers, including Swiss priest Ulrich Zwingli and French religious thinker John Calvin, joined him in calling for the church to cease various corrupt practices. Among them were buying and selling church offices; over-indulgence in luxury by leading churchmen; clergymen keeping mistresses; lack of discipline in monasteries; and numerous others.

These and other reformers soon broke free of the Catholic Church. In what came to be called the Reformation, they established new branches of Christianity that collectively came to be called "Protestant" (because they were born out

A lithograph depicting Martin Luther burning the Papal Bull excommunicating him from the Rom[an] Catholic Church, along with vignettes from Luther's life and portraits of other religious reformers[.]

Heroes of the Reformation!

of protests against the existing church). By the time that Luther passed away in 1546, at least half of all Europeans belonged to Protestant denominations, including Lutherans, Calvinists, Anglicans, and others.

These new kinds of Christians viewed themselves as products of a new age. And they were right. The permanent fragmentation of the medieval church, one of that age's greatest institutions and symbols, is one of several seminal events that historians have proposed to mark the end of the Middle Ages.

Chapter Eight:
Explorers and Thinkers Expand Europe's Horizons

The increasing divisions in and eventual breakup of the medieval church was only one of the factors marking the transition from the medieval era to the modern one. Historians have singled out others, including the demise of the manorial system; expanded trade and banking that hastened the shift from a land-based to money-based economy; the emergence of highly centralized, modern-style nations; and the introduction of the printing press and other technological advances.

To these factors must be added two more. First was the Renaissance, which began in Italy in the 1300s and steadily spread to other parts of Europe. The Renaissance was a period of intellectual awakening in which European thinkers developed new ways of viewing nature, society, and humanity's place in the scheme of things. Part of this awakening included the beginnings of scientific thought. Another aspect of it was a growing emphasis on the value and potential of the individual human being. The idea that all people are worthy encouraged the rise of more enlightened political institutions and expanded educational opportunities. It also helped to drive the outburst of individual artistic expression that characterized the Renaissance.

The other factor that contributed to the waning of the Middle Ages was the inception of the great age of exploration. Beginning in the 1400s, navigators from Portugal, Spain, England, Italy, and other European lands discovered entire new continents. This opened up fantastic new realms of knowledge and economic opportunities. Indeed, the medieval mindset had long been insular, or inward-looking. From its inception, it had been built almost entirely around Europe-centered heritage, customs, politics, and ideas. Then, in the span of only a few years, Europeans were forced to accept a host of momentous new realities about the world. As the noted scholar and archaeologist John R. Hale explained:

> The discovery of new lands many times greater in extent than Europe itself [spurred] the development of systematic [orderly] exploration; the [separation] of geographic facts from age-old myths, [causing] a major break with medieval patterns of thought; the modification of a good deal of medieval religious, political, and social [ideas]; and, as a long-term result, a realignment of political power in Europe.

The Power of Reason

Even before explorers began to expand Europe's horizons beyond the oceans, some thinkers and creative individuals had started to change the way Europeans saw the world. In the 1100s and 1200s, Europe's educated classes rediscovered the writings and ideas of Aristotle, Cicero, and other ancient classical (Greco-Roman) thinkers. The writings covered a wide variety of intellectual disciplines, including astronomy, botany, geometry, mechanics, and rhetoric (the art of persuasive speaking).

The ancient knowledge came to be seen as more than merely admirable. Many late medieval Europeans felt that the lost Greco-Roman civilization was superior to their own. In the mid-1300s the Italian scholar and thinker Francesco Petrarch wrote:

Better would it had been if we had been born far
earlier or far later. There was once, and their may
be again, a happier time. This present age holds
[nothing] but sordidness, [for] wisdom and virtue
and the love of glory have fled the world, where
now dishonor rules. . . . Unless we rise again by
mighty effort, soon for us the end will come.

Petrarch and his contemporaries strongly believed that the
classical world and its ideas should be imitated. So they duti-
fully incorporated the ancient writings into the lessons taught
in the universities that were appearing in increasing numbers
across Europe in the 1200s and 1300s.

Intrigued and strongly influenced by the philosophical
ideas in these writings, several teachers, writers, and other
liberal thinkers began building on them. This generated much
of the intellectual energy that fueled the opening decades of
the Renaissance. As a result, that unusually productive period
witnessed fresh approaches to viewing government, society,
the arts, and how people might best express themselves and
achieve their full potential.

Most of all, there was a growing recognition of an important
truth first articulated by the ancient Greeks. Namely, human
beings possess an inherent dignity and worth. Furthermore,
medieval people were perfectly capable of uncovering whatever truths remained to be discovered about life and the
universe. In this view, there was no need to call upon mysti-
cal or divine forces to find these truths. Rather, all that was
needed were the existing tools provided by the human mind
and character—reason, logic, curiosity, persistence, and independent thinking.

Because this argument extolled innate human virtues,
the Renaissance thinkers who advanced it called themselves
humanists (from the Latin word *humanitas*, meaning "humanity"). Among the foremost Renaissance humanists were Italy's
Petrarch (born in 1304), Giovanni Boccaccio (1313), Leonardo
Bruni (1374), and Giovanni Pico della Mirandola (1463);
the Netherlands' Desiderius Erasmus (1466); England's

Thomas More (1478); Spain's Juan Luis Vives (1493); and France's François Rabelais (1495).

Through these individuals, scholar G. R. Elton remarked, "the transmitted experience of the ancient world was married to independent thought and direct experience to produce a genuine liberation of the human spirit." In a sense, the humanists advocated joining that free spirit with the mental power of reason. This was the basis for free inquiry into nature and the expansion of knowledge, which, the humanists pointed out, could be exploited for society's benefit. By consistently following this approach, they held, humans could become the masters of their own destiny.

Yet while the Renaissance humanists promoted scientific inquiry and other secular activities, they remained, like most other medieval Europeans, deeply religious. In their view, God had endowed them and other humans with extraordinary mental tools. It therefore followed that God both expected and wanted them to use these tools. In fact, the humanists argued, employing their God-given gifts to expand knowledge about the world and the way it works actually *glorified* God, rather than disrespected him.

A portrait of Thomas More by Hans Holbein the Younger, circa 1527. Thomas More wrote the novel *Utopia*, which idealizes a communistic political system, religious toleration, and equality among peoples.

The Benefits of Free Will

One of the classic statements of the concept that humans possess the inherent ability to shape their own destiny was made by Italian humanist Giovanni Pico della Mirandola in his *Oration on the Dignity of Man.*

At last it seems to me I have come to understand why man is the most fortunate of creatures and consequently worthy of all admiration. [It] is on this very account that man is rightly called and judged a great miracle and a wonderful creature indeed. [God told humanity:] "You, [who are] constrained [held back] by no limits, in accordance with your own free will, in whose hand I have placed you, shall ordain for yourself the limits of your nature. . . . With freedom of choice, [you] may fashion yourself in whatever shape you shall prefer.". . . O highest and most marvelous felicity [happiness] of man! To him it is granted [by God] to have whatever he chooses, to be whatever he wills!

The Original Renaissance Men

The humanists and other creative individuals during the Renaissance felt that God had given people more than the ability to learn about existing natural facts and wonders. Some people had also been endowed with the talent to create new wonders of their own. One result of the new, more liberal atmosphere in Europe, therefore, was a huge cultural outburst in the arts, especially architecture, painting, and sculpture.

Many of the architects who came to the fore were "civic humanists." Their main goal was to work with government officials and wealthy local citizens to make their home cities not only more beautiful but also better able to compete with or outshine other cities. The case of Florence, one of Europe's most populous and powerful cities, was illustrative. There, the civic humanist Leon Battista Alberti (born in 1404) designed several new structures while adding to some existing ones. One of his finest achievements was a new façade (decorative exterior) for the church of Santa Maria Novella.

Alberti's splendid additions to the building reflect a major characteristic of Renaissance architecture—a look of balance and symmetry. It was achieved in part by making the various design elements conform to mathematical ratios expressed in whole numbers, for example 1 to 2 and 2 to 4. At the time, the prevailing view was that such ratios existed in nature, having been placed there by God. Using them in an artificial structure would help to give it the appearance of natural beauty. Alberti stated:

> There is a certain excellence and natural beauty
> in the figures and forms of buildings [that] strikes
> the mind with pleasure and admiration. [It is a
> sense of harmony that derives] from nature, so
> that its true seat is in the mind and in reason.
> This is what architecture chiefly aims at, and by
> this she obtains her beauty, dignity, and value.

Alberti attempted to apply this principle of harmony and proportion to his other creative works as well. In addition to his architectural endeavors, he was also a gifted painter, musician, and poet. He exemplified the multitalented individual that later came to be called the "Renaissance man," after the period in which he lived. An even more renowned Renaissance man, Leonardo da Vinci (born in 1452) was also an Italian. His accomplishments as a sculptor, painter, engineer, and inventor became legendary in later centuries. His somewhat younger countrymen, Michelangelo Buonarotti (1475), another enormously versatile individual, is now seen as the Renaissance's supreme artist. The paintings he did of the biblical creation on the ceiling of Rome's Sistine Chapel are universally recognized to be among the two or three finest artistic achievements that Europe ever produced.

Michelangelo's Extraordinary Talents

Michelangelo Buonarotti (1475-1564) was born in a small town in northern Italy and grew up in Florence. Even as a child he demonstrated extraordinary artistic talents, which were realized later in his many masterpieces. Of these, the most famous is the collection of paintings gracing the ceiling of the Sistine Chapel, in the Vatican, completed in 1512. As tremendous as this achievement was, it was but one of many creative projects Michelangelo tackled in his long life. Among them were some of the greatest sculptures ever produced, including a colossal statue of the biblical character David (1504), and the exquisite *Pietà* (1499), depicting the recently crucified Jesus cradled by his mother, Mary. Michelangelo also designed the dome for Saint Peter's Basilica in Rome and the Laurentian Library in Florence's San Lorenzo church.

Michelangelo's *David*

The World Transformed

In 1483, when Leonardo was thirty-one and Michelangelo was only eight, Portuguese navigators sailed to the mouth of the Congo River in western Africa. A few decades before, leading Portuguese mariners had set out to explore that mysterious continent's coasts. Their ultimate goal was to find a way around Africa to the Indian Ocean. That would hopefully allow their nation to exploit the vast and lucrative markets of China, India, and other legendary lands of the Far East. They were well on their way to accomplishing that goal when Portugal's Bartholomew Dias sailed around the Cape of Good Hope, on Africa's southern tip, in 1488.

This string of bold and risky adventures set the stage, so to speak, for a long and historic series of global voyages by explorers from several European countries. Some, like the Portuguese, aimed to reach eastern Asia by sailing eastward. Others were determined to find a shorter route to these lands by traveling westward into the Atlantic Ocean.

The first of those who advocated sailing west to achieve success was Christopher Columbus, an Italian sailing for Spain. In 1492, only four years after Dias's historic trip around southern Africa, Columbus crossed the Atlantic and landed in a group of lush islands. At first, he assumed that these were situated near the coast of India. So he called the local natives Indians (a name that stuck and remains in use today). In the years that followed, however, it became clear that Columbus had come upon two formerly unknown and immense continents (later dubbed North and South America).

Numerous others followed Columbus in the waning years of the medieval era. In fact, collectively speaking these voyages became one of the principal causes of the medieval era's demise. By opening up enormous new territories for economic exploitation and eventually settlement by Europeans, the explorers in a very real sense replaced the old, inward-looking

Europe with a new outward-looking one. And in so doing, they opened the way for a bustling global society that saw, and still sees, itself as "modern." John Hale elaborates:

> The urge to find new lands beyond Europe led to an unprecedented increase in knowledge about this planet. Discovery led to colonization and settlement, to overseas commitments that influenced the rise and fall of nations in Europe. It brought new wealth, new products, new opportunities, new problems, new ways of thinking. It led to the creation of new nations, the United States among them.

By the mid-to-late 1500s, therefore, Europe had left its Middle Ages behind, another relic in the growing heap of bygone eras. Medieval Europeans had made an indelible mark, however, not only on their own continent, but on the world as well. C. Warren Hollister points out:

> Anyone who wonders how Western Europe managed to transform the world, for good or ill, into the global civilization that envelopes us today must look to the medieval centuries for an important part of the answer. For during the Middle Ages, Europe grew from a predominantly rural society, thinly settled and impoverished, into a powerful and distinctive civilization. . . . During the "modern" centuries that followed, [European] fleets, armies, and ideas spread across the globe and transformed it.

That transformation, which proved in some ways beneficial, and in others less so, helped to make the world what it is today.

This 1893 illustration romanticizes Christopher Columbus's landing in North America.

✿ Timeline

476	Traditional date for the fall of the western Roman Empire.
565	Death of the eastern Roman (or Byzantine) emperor Justinian
732	The Frankish war leader Charles Martel defeats an invading Muslim army in central France.
751	Pepin the Short becomes king of the Franks.
768	Charlemagne ascends the Frankish throne.
793	The first major Viking raid in western Europe occurs at Lindisfarne, on Britain's eastern coast.
800	Charlemagne is crowned "Emperor of the Romans."
ca. 800-ca. 1200	Europe experiences unusually warm temperatures during the so-called Medieval Warming Period (MWP).
814	Charlemagne dies and is succeeded by Louis the Pious.
846	Rome is plundered by Muslim pirates.
885	An army of Vikings raids Paris.
1066	Norman leader William the Conqueror crosses the English Channel and defeats the Anglo-Saxons in the battle of Hasting
1095	Pope Urban II calls for Europe's nobles to go to Palestine to capture Jerusalem from the Muslims then administering it.
1295	England's King Edward I calls representatives of all social classes to meet in what becomes known as the Model Parliament.
1304	Birth of the Renaissance humanist Francesco Petrarch.
1309	Pope Clement V moves the papal offices to the French town of Avignon.
1315-1317	The Great Famine, caused by a decline in food production, kills millions of Europeans.

1337	The Hundred Years' War, fought between England and France, begins.
1346	The English defeat the French in the battle of Crecy.
1347-1354	The Black Death, now known to be bubonic plague, sweeps through the Middle East and Europe.
1358	Thousands of French peasants rebel and burn estates of wealthy nobles.
1431	During the Hundred Years' War, female French war leader Joan of Arc is captured by the English and burned at the stake.
1453	The Hundred Years' War ends; Johann Gutenberg introduces the first printing press using movable type.
1469	Isabella, queen of Castile, marries Ferdinand, king of Aragon, forming the nucleus of the nation of Spain.
1475	Birth of the great sculptor, painter, and architect Michelangelo.
1488	Portuguese navigator Bartholomew Dias sails around the southern tip of Africa.
1492	Sailing for Spain, Italian-born mariner Christopher Columbus lands in the West Indies, initiating a great age of global exploration.
1517	German monk Martin Luther levels serious charges against the Catholic Church, initiating the Reformation.

✿ Sources

CHAPTER ONE:
The Emergence of Medieval Europe

p. 9,   "The cities which survived . . ." Thomas Brown, "The
          Transformation of the Roman Mediterranean, 400-900," in
          George Holmes, ed. *The Oxford History of Medieval Europe*
          (New York: Oxford University Press, 1989), 26.

p. 10,   "The end of the world . . ." Brian Tierney, ed., *The Middle
          Ages: Volume I, Sources of Medieval History* (New York:
          Knopf, 1998), 65.

p. 11,   "The entire Mediterranean Sea . . ." Naphtali Lewis, *Life in
          Egypt Under Roman Rule* (Atlanta: Scholar's Press, 1999), 11.

p. 15,   "filled the power vacuum . . ." Justo L. Gonzalez, *The Story of
          Christianity, Volume I, The Early Church to the Dawn of the
          Reformation* (New York: Harper One, 2010), 218.

p. 15,   "and began to urge him . . ." Gregory of Tours, *History of
          the Franks*, trans. Ernest Brehaut (New York: Norton, 1969),
          40-41.

p. 16,   "The blending of Roman . . ." C. Warren Hollister, *Medieval
          Europe: A Short History* (New York: McGraw-Hill, 1998), 60.

p. 17,   "large and robust . . ." Einhard, *Life of Charlemagne*,
          excerpted in Norman F. Cantor, *The Medieval Reader* (New
          York: HarperCollins, 1994), 101.

p. 19,   "The Christian religion . . ." Ibid, 102.

CHAPTER TWO:
Manors, Castles, Lords, and Peasants

p. 23,   "Our community lay prostrate . . ." Naphtali Lewis and Meyer
          Reinhold, eds., *Roman Civilization, Sourcebook II: The
          Empire* (New York: Harper and Row, 1966), 478.

p. 24,   "Any person whatsoever . . ." Ibid, 483.

p. 24,   "Virtually serfs . . ." Michael Grant, *A Social History of Greece and Rome* (New York: Scribner's, 1992), 90-91.

p. 24,   "The central government . . ." Harold Mattingly, *The Man on the Roman Street* (New York: Norton, 1980), 147.

p. 27,   "In the upper story . . ."

p. 27,   "Outside of [the manor house is] . . ." Tierney, *The Middle Ages, Volume I*, 283-284.

p. 28,   "was content with his lot," Morris Bishop, *The Middle Ages* (Boston: Mariner, 2001), 233.

p. 29,   "Hugh Miller holds . . ." Tierney, *The Middle Ages, Volume I*, 285.

p. 33,   "Castles thus fostered . . ." Hollister, *Medieval Europe*, 126.

p. 34,   "The period continues to exercise . . ." Jeffrey L. Singman, *Daily Life in Medieval Europe* (Westport, CT: Greenwood Press, 1999), ix.

CHAPTER THREE:
The Growth of Nation-states

p. 37,   "[The Vikings] created . . ." John Haywood, *The Penguin Historical Atlas of the Vikings* (New York: Penguin, 1995), 20.

p. 37,   "From the fury of the Northmen . . ." Howard La Fay, *The Vikings* (Washington, DC: National Geographic, 1972), 8.

p. 39,   "The heathens . . ." James Ingram, trans., *Anglo-Saxon Chronicle*, Online Medieval and Classical Library, http://omacl.org/Anglo/part2.html.

p. 40,   "The King [rode] . . ." Ibid.

pp. 40-42, "The enemy had not . . ." Ibid.

p. 42, "The invasions had the effect . . ." Hollister, *Medieval Europe*, 119.

p. 43, "The Norman kings discovered . . ." Ibid, 251.

p. 44, "The increasingly important towns . . ." Donald Kagan, *The Western Heritage*, 1300-1815 (New York: Macmillan,1983), 361.

p. 45, "The political and social consequences . . ." Ibid, 345.

p. 48, "In their separate ways . . ." Anne Fremantle, *Age of Faith* (New York: Time-Life, 1979), 141.

CHAPTER FOUR:
The Rise of Towns and Urban Life

p. 50, "A town was distinguished . . ." Singman, *Daily Life in Medieval Europe*, 174.

p. 52, "On the riverbank . . ." Cantor, *The Medieval Reader*, 69.

p. 54, "Inadequate drainage meant . . ." Singman, *Daily Life in Medieval Europe*, 188-189.

p. 55, "The dignity and office . . ." Tierney, *The Middle Ages, Volume I*, 359.

p. 56, "Beware of eating too much . . ." Leon Bernard and Theodore B. Hodges, eds., *Readings in European History* (New York: Macmillan, 1961), 147-148.

p. 61, "She ought to ensure . . ." Cantor, *The Medieval Reader*, 230.

p. 61, "I had them . . ." Geoffrey Chaucer, "The Wife of Bath's Tale," trans. Gerard NeCastro, http://www.umm.maine.edu/faculty/necastro/chaucer/translation/ct/07wbt.pdf.

p. 62, "All [male] inhabitants . . ." Marjorie Rowling, *Life in Medieval Times* (New York: Dorset, 1987), 72-73.

CHAPTER FIVE:
Knights, Crusaders, and Warfare

p. 64,   "expel that wicked . . ." Tierney, *The Middle Ages, Volume I*, 156.

p. 66,   "With trumpets sounding . . ." Bernard and Hodges, *Readings in European History*, 103.

p. 67,   "Two centuries of death . . ." James A. Haught, *Holy Horrors* (New York: Prometheus, 1990), 27.

p. 67,   "It is this Western desire . . ." Victor Davis Hanson, *The Western Way of War* (New York: University of California Press, 2009), 9, 14.

p. 68,   "The sharp [English] arrows . . ." Bernard and Hodges, *Readings in European History*, 177.

p. 70,   "Knight, God grant you . . ." Rowling, *Life in Medieval Times*, 40.

p. 71,   "An individual with military power . . ." Singman, *Daily Life in Medieval Europe*, 5.

p. 72,   "Vassalage was not . . ." Melissa Snell, "The F-Word, Page Six," http://historymedren.about.com/od/feudalism/a/feudalism_cont.htm.

p. 76,   "The whole of Italy . . ." John Keegan, *A History of Warfare* (New York: Vintage, 1993), 321.

CHAPTER SIX:
Ravaged by Famine and Plague

p. 79,   "There was no governmental organization . . ." Bishop, *The Middle Ages*, 373.

p. 79,   "Hunger grew in the land . . ." Tierney, *The Middle Ages, Volume I*, 329-330.

p. 80,   "Nothing like it . . ." Jean de Venette, Chronicle, in *The Black Death*, ed. Rosemary Horrox (Manchester, England: Manchester University Press, 1994), 5.

p. 82,   "the plague almost closed . . ." David Herlihy, *The Black Death and the Transformation of the West* (Cambridge, MA: Harvard University Press, 1997), 25.

p. 82,   "See how England mourns . . ." Anonymous, in *The Black Death*, ed. Rosemary Horrox, 126.

p. 82,   "become putrid or corrupt . . ." *Report of the Paris Medical Faculty, October 1348*, 161.

p. 82,   "No one [shall] dare . . ." *Anti-plague Ordinances of Pistoia, 1348*, 195-196.

p. 83,   "All the Jews . . ." Heinrich Truchess von Diessenhoven, "The Persecution of the Jews," in *The Black Death*, ed. Rosemary Horrox, 208-209.

p. 84,   "In the second half . . ." Philip Ziegler, *The Black Death* (New York: Harper Perennial, 2009), 228.

p. 84,   "The world [is going] . . ." Otto Friedrich, *The End of the World: A History* (New York: Fromm International, 1994), 135.

p. 85,   "With staves . . ." Tierney, *The Middle Ages, Volume I*, 339.

p. 87,   "As long as wages were low . . ." Herlihy, *The Black Death and the Transformation of the West*, 50.

CHAPTER SEVEN:
Mounting Divisions in the Church

p. 90,   "By the late ninth century . . ." Brown, "The Transformation of the Roman Mediterranean," 45.

p. 91,   "traveled in ships . . ." Cantor, *The Medieval Reader*, 52.

p. 91,   "Early in life . . ." Ibid.

p. 91,   "built an excellent shelter . . ." Ibid.

p. 92,   "was filled with . . ." Hollister, *Medieval Europe*, 68-69.

p. 94,   "[In hell] murderers . . ." Edward E. Foster, ed., "The Vision of Tundale: Introduction," http://www.lib.rochester.edu/camelot/teams/vtint.htm..

pp. 94-95, "may be permitted . . ." Tierney, *The Middle Ages, Volume I*, 142-143.

p. 95,   "false monk . . ." Ibid., 144-145.

p. 96,   "After Boniface's humiliation . . ." Kagan, *The Western Heritage*, 353.

p. 97,   "Abandoning much . . ." Hollister, *Medieval Europe*, 334-335.

CHAPTER EIGHT:
Explorers and Thinkers Expand Europe's Horizons

p. 102,   "The discovery of new lands . . ." John R. Hale, *Age of Exploration* (New York: Time-Life, 1979), 161.

p. 103,   "Better would it have been . . ." Cantor, *The Medieval Reader,* 311.

p. 104,   "the transmitted experience . . ." G. R. Elton, *Renaissance and Reformation, 1300-1648* (New York: Macmillan, 1976), 47.

p. 105,   "At last it seems . . ." Giovanni Pico della Mirandola, *Oration on the Dignity of Man*, in Karl F. Thompson, ed., *Middle Ages, Renaissance, and Reformation* (New York: Harcourt, Brace and World, 1964), 185-186.

p. 106,   "There is a certain excellence . . ." H. W. Janson and Anthony F. Janson, *History of Art* (New York: Harry N. Abrams, 1997), 630.

p. 109,   "The urge to find . . ." Hale, *Age of Exploration*, 11.

p. 109,   "Anyone who wonders . . ." Hollister, *Medieval Europe*, 1-2.

✿ Bibliography

Selected Books

Arnold, Thomas F. *The Renaissance at War*. London: Cassell, 2001.

Atchity, Kenneth J., ed. *The Renaissance Reader*. New York: HarperCollins, 1996.

Bartlett, Robert. *The Making of Europe: Conquest, Colonization and Cultural Change*, 950-1350. Princeton: Princeton University Press, 1993.

Bishop, Morris. *The Middle Ages*. Boston: Mariner, 2001.

Brown, Peter. *The World of Late Antiquity, A.D. 150-750*. New York: Norton, 1989.

Cantor, Norman F. *The Medieval Reader*. New York: HarperCollins, 1994.

Chartrand, Rene. *The Vikings: Voyagers of Discovery and Plunder*. Oxford, Eng.: Osprey, 2006.

Gies, Joseph, and Frances Gies. *Life in a Medieval City*. New York: Harper and Row, 1981.

Gonzalez, Justo L. *The Story of Christianity, Volume I, The Early Church to the Dawn of the Reformation*. San Francisco: Harper and Row, 1984.

Gravett, Christopher. Hastings *1066: The Fall of Saxon England*. Oxford, Eng.: Osprey, 1992.

Hall, Richard. *The World of the Vikings*. London: Thames and Hudson, 2007.

Herlihy, David. *The Black Death and the Transformation of the West*. Edited by Samuel K. Cohn, Jr. Cambridge, MA: Harvard University Press, 1997.

Hollister, C. Warren. *Medieval Europe: A Short History*. New York: McGraw-Hill, 1998.

Holmes, George, ed. *The Oxford History of Medieval Europe*. New York: Oxford University Press, 1989.

Hooper, Nicholas, and Matthew Bennett. *The Cambridge Illustrated Atlas of Warfare: The Middle Ages, 768-1487.* New York: Cambridge University Press, 1996.

Horrox, Rosemary, ed. *The Black Death.* Manchester, Eng.: Manchester University Press, 1994.

Huppert, George. *After the Black Death: A Social History of Early Modern Europe.* Bloomington: Indiana University Press, 1998.

Jones, Archer. *The Art of War in the Western World.* New York: Oxford University Press, 1987.

Kauffman, H. W. *The Medieval Fortress: Castles, Forts, and Walled Cities of the Middle Ages.* New York: Da Capo Press, 2004.

Langford, Jerome J. *Galileo, Science, and the Church.* Ann Arbor: University of Michigan Press, 1992.

McKitterick, Rosamond. *Atlas of the Medieval World.* London: Oxford University Press, 2004.

McManners, John, ed. *The Oxford History of Christianity.* Oxford: Oxford University Press, 1990.

Randers-Pehrson, Justine D. *Barbarians and Romans: The Birth Struggle of Europe, A.D. 400-700.* Norman, OK: University of Oklahoma Press, 1983.

Rowling, Marjorie. *Life in Medieval Times.* New York: Dorset, 1987.

Southern, R.W. *The Making of the Middle Ages.* London: Folio Society, 2000.

Tierney, Brian, ed. *The Middle Ages: Volume I, Sources of Medieval History.* New York: Knopf, 1973.

Toy, Sidney. *Castles: Their Construction and History.* New York: Dover, 1984.

Tuchman, Barbara W. *A Distant Mirror: The Calamitous 14th Century.* New York: Ballantine, 1996.

White Lynn, Jr. *Medieval Technology and Social Change.* London: Oxford University Press, 1981.

Wise, Terence. *Medieval European Armies.* Oxford, Eng.: Osprey, 2000.

❀ Web sites

The Black Death
http://www.insecta-inspecta.com/fleas/bdeath/bdeath.html

The Crusades
http://www.medieval-life-and-times.info/crusades/index.htm

Intellectual History in the High Middle Ages
http://cliojournal.wikispaces.com/Intellectual+Activity+in+the+High+Middle+Ages

Internet Medieval Sourcebook
http://www.fordham.edu/halsall/sbook1i.html

Medieval Life and the Hundred Years' War.
http://www.hyw.com/books/history/1_Help_C.htm

Medieval Manor
http://mars.wnec.edu/~grempel/courses/wc1/lectures/22manor.html

Medieval Monks
www.historyforkids.org/learn/medieval/people/monks.htm

Medieval Women
www.mw.mcmaster.ca/home.html

Michelangelo Buonarroti
www.michelangelo.com/buonarroti.html

The Papacy of Innocent III
http://cliojournal.wikispaces.com/The+Papacy+of+Innocent+III

People of the Middle Ages
http://www.themiddleages.net/people_middle_ages.html

Secrets of Norse Ships
www.pbs.org/wgbh/nova/vikings/ships.html

Significance of the Stirrup in Medieval Warfare
http://cliojournal.wikispaces.com/Significance+of+the+Stirrup+in+Medieval+Warfare

The Vikings
www.viking.no/e/index.html

🔅 Glossary

bailiff: On a medieval estate, a manager in charge of peasant workers.

ballista: A large spear throwing device that medieval armies borrowed from the Greeks and Romans.

cavalry (or cavalrymen): Mounted soldiers.

clergy: Bishops, priests, monks, and other churchmen.

coloni (singular *colonus*): In late Roman times, poor farmers tied to life and work on wealthy estates.

Danegold: A large amount of money or valuables given to a Viking band as a bribe to keep its members from raiding and killing.

feudal relationship: In mid-to-late medieval times, a mutual agreement between a wealthy noble and a follower in which the former gave the latter land in return for military service.

fief: In feudal arrangements, the land given to the vassal by the lord.

flagellants: During the onset of the Black Death, people who whipped and otherwise punished themselves to persuade God to end the plague.

flying buttress: In a Gothic structure, a partial stone arch erected outside to help support the weight of the building's upper sections.

Gothic: An medieval architectural style characterized by the use of tall stain glass windows, flying buttresses, and towering spires.

hall (or great hall): The principal living space in a medieval house or castle.

guild: In medieval times, a union-like trade organization that looked after the interests of its members in both their jobs and private lives.

humanism: In Europe's Renaissance, an intellectual movement whose members advocated the inherent worth and dignity of human beings.

infantry (or infantrymen): Foot soldiers.

mail (or chain-mail): A flexible kind of armor consisting of a mesh of metal rings sewn onto a stiff shirt.

manor: An estate owned by a medieval nobleman.

manor house: The home of the owner of a manor.

manorial system: The medieval arrangement in which serfs and other workers farmed portions of a manor and in return performed various services for the owner.

moat: A ditch dug around a castle or town to help fend off attackers.

monastic movement: The spread of monasteries in which monks led simple lives of self-denial.

monk: In medieval times, a churchman who lived and worked in a monastery.

motte-and-bailey: An early version of a medieval castle, built mainly of wood atop a low hill (the motte).

papal: Having to do with the popes of the Roman Catholic Church.

peasant: A poor agricultural worker.

pike: A long spear wielded by formations of medieval soldiers (most often Swiss and Scots).

reeve: On a medieval English estate, a peasant foreman who kept watch over his fellow workers.

Reformation: The period beginning in 1517 in which the Catholic Church fragmented, producing numerous Protestant denominations.

Renaissance: A period of the late Middle Ages that witnessed an outburst of spectacular intellectual and artistic achievements.

sap: A tunnel dug under a castle's wall during a siege.

secular: Non-spiritual or non-religious.

serf: A medieval peasant tied to life and work on a nobleman's estate.

shell keep: A stone tower that replaced motte-and-baileys in the evolution of medieval castles.

steward (or seneschal): The general supervisor of a medieval manner.

thatch: Bundled twigs or plant stems used for roofs and other parts of medieval cottages.

trebuchet: A large catapult-like weapon used in medieval warfare, especially sieges of castles.

urban: Having to do with towns and cities and life in them.

vassal: In the feudal relationship, a person who received land from a nobleman and owed that lord loyalty and military service in return.

wattle-and-daub: A primitive building technique featuring interwoven branches plastered with clay, dung, and other materials.

🙰 Index

✼ Picture Credits